T0102078

Strength
of Soul

Strength
of Soul

Naomi Raquel Enright

FLORIDA ■ NEW YORK
www.2leafpress.org

2LEAF PRESS INC.
New York Offices
P.O. Box 4378
Grand Central Station
New York, New York 10163-4378
editor@2leafpress.org

2LEAF PRESS INC. is a
nonprofit 501(c)(3) organization that promotes
multicultural literature and literacy.
Stephanie Ann Agosto, Executive Director
www.2lpinc.org

Copyright © 2019 Naomi Raquel Enright

Cover art: Sebastián Whittaker
Cover design: Adam Whittaker
Book design and layout: Gabrielle David
Copy Editor: Carolina Fung Feng

Library of Congress Control Number: 2017963102

ISBN-13: 978-1-940939-72-8 (Paperback)
ISBN-13: 978-1-940939-85-8 (eBook)

10   9   8   7   6   5   4   3   2   1

Published in the United States of America

First Edition | First Printing

2Leaf Press trade distribution is handled by University of Chicago Press / Chicago Distribution Center (www.press.uchicago.edu) 773.702.7010. Titles are also available for corporate, premium, and special sales. Please direct inquiries to the UCP Sales Department, 773.702.7248.

Para Sebastián

❧ ❦

*And dedicated to my family
past, present and future*

Ever since my father died, as I have adjusted to life without his physical presence, the sun has shone in moments I have missed him most. I genuinely feel my father's presence in the sun and it has always managed not only to bring me light, but to give me strength. Having my son paint this art symbolizes that he too is my light and my strength and that bringing him into the world is the catalyst for this book.

"When someone with the authority of a teacher, say, describes the world and you are not in it, there is a moment of psychic disequilibrium, as if you looked into a mirror and saw nothing. Yet you know you exist and others like you, that this is a game done with mirrors. It takes some strength of soul–and not just individual strength, but collective understanding–to resist this void...and to stand up, demanding to be seen and heard."

—Adrienne Rich,
Blood, Bread, and Poetry: Selected Prose (1979-1985)

CONTENTS

PREFACE

WHEN MY SON OPENED HIS EYES for the first time in December 2010 and my father's permanently closed in November 2011, I was thrust into a reexamination of my identity. I was now a mother and a fatherless daughter.

My light-skinned, blond, blue/green-eyed son reminded me in many ways of the beloved father I had lost, and as I adjusted to my new normal, I began to take stock of my history and of my future.

As I took stock, I thought a great deal about the racism and erasure I have experienced my entire life as a bilingual, multiethnic, multi-citizenship individual living in the United States. The transformative experience of bringing my son into the world and saying goodbye to the father who had in part produced us both propelled me to truly examine systemic racism and its perpetuation.

My son needs to see his story reflected in the printed word. It is only through seeing his family's complex history reflected that he will be able to see himself—and others—in totality.

Our stories are not written on our faces. ❊

ACKNOWLEDGMENTS

THIS BOOK WOULD NOT have been possible without my publisher, Gabrielle David at 2Leaf Press. Thank you, Gabrielle, for publishing my first essay, "From One Exile To Another" in the anthology *The Beiging of America* (2017), and thank you for believing in me.

Thank you to my friend, Geraldine Woods, who was the first person to tell me I "had a book in me." Your belief in my writing gave me the courage to share my story. *Un fuerte abrazo.*

I wish to thank Manhattan Country School and Horace Mann School. I would not have written this book without the change and growth I experienced in both schools.

I will be forever grateful to the National SEED Project and to all of the mentors and colleagues I met as a result. SEED absolutely reconstructed my soul.

Thank you to my advance readers and blurb writers, all of whom are being the change in their own spheres and who inspire me every day. Thank you for saying "yes."

There are not enough words, in either of my languages, to express the love, respect and gratitude I feel for my *autores,*

Joseph H. and Pilar Alava Enright. You both gave me the gift of life as well as the strength to live on my own terms. I miss you every day, Daddy.

Thank you to my brother, Nicky Enright, who shared the fortune of having such wonderful parents with me and who inspires me to speak truth to power. *Te quiero mucho, ñaño.*

Thank you to my *familia extendida*, in the United States and in Ecuador. I am so blessed to have grown up with such a boisterous, humorous and supportive family. All of you are my home. *Los quiero mucho.*

Thank you to my *familia política*, in Ohio, Indiana and in Georgia. Without all of you, I would not have my husband and son, and I thank you for welcoming me into your family.

Thank you to my ancestors, spread throughout the globe, all of whom contributed to my existence. I carry all of you within me.

Thank you to my friends, in the United States and abroad, without whose friendship I could not have the drive to be the change I want to see. I love you all.

I have saved my most profound gratitude for my husband, Adam Whittaker and for my son, Sebastián Whittaker. The two of you are my anchors and I am so blessed to be your wife and your mother.

Amor, I will always be thankful to you for loving me as I am, and for choosing to swim against the tide alongside me. I love you.

Sebastián, me has ensanchado el corazón y me has expandido la visión. Te adoro, mi maravilla. ❁

Naomi Raquel Enright

ONE

Is That Your Real Dad?

MY STORY BEGINS February 6, 1978 in La Paz, Bolivia. I was born to an American father and an Ecuadorian mother. My father, Joseph Hill Enright, born May 18, 1940 in Syracuse, New York, descended from Eastern European (Ashkenazi) Jews and my mother, Pilar Alejandrina Alava Mestanza, born April 21, 1946 in Guayaquil, Ecuador, descended from West African, Native American and Spanish ancestors. My parents met in February 1965, when my father was a Peace Corps volunteer teaching English in Guayaquil and my mother was one of his students. They were married in Guayaquil on September 2, 1967, and were married for forty-four years until my father's death on November 29, 2011.

Three months prior to my parents' wedding, on June 12, 1967, interracial marriage became legal in the United States. The Supreme Court ruled in *Loving v. Virginia* that it was unconstitutional to criminalize miscegenation. There were states prior to 1967 where it had never been illegal to marry someone of a "different race," but the *Loving* decision made interracial marriage legal in the entire country.

It has always moved me that my parents married the same year that such a historic, monumental decision was made. Although my parents were not married in this country, prior to 1967, their marriage would have been illegal and considered amoral in much of the United States. The fact that a marriage like theirs was recognized and affirmed by the United States Supreme Court the very same year they got married has always felt invigorating and empowering to me. I know my parents did not belong to "different races," but the fact is that many did and do believe that they were in an interracial marriage, so *Loving* has always meant a lot to me. I have also loved that the couple who brought the case against Virginia had the last name "Loving." It was pure coincidence, but a serendipitous and powerful one.

Terms such as "interracial," "different races," and "miscegenation" are preposterous. There is no scientific basis for these terms (and many others), which are nothing more than made-up labels that have been used to define and separate people for millennia. Racial namings is more than a social construct, it reflects the cultural attitudes of imperial powers dominant during the age of European colonial expansion. In fact, modern scholarship views these racial namings and categories as socially constructed, that is, race is not intrinsic to human beings but rather an identity created, often by socially dominant groups, to establish meaning in a social context. This often involves the suppression of groups defined as racially inferior, as in the one-drop rule used in the nineteenth-century to exclude those with any amount of African ancestry from the dominant racial grouping, defined as "white." Of course, in order to validate these namings, scientists like Samuel Morton gave racism legitimacy. Journalists, and teachers popularized their findings, going so far as to preach white supremacy, which unfortunately, many people believe to this day. It has been scientifically proven time and again, however, that there is not a single absolute genetic difference between human beings. (Kolbert, 2018)

Interestingly, the term "Hispanic," an ethnonym adopted during the Nixon administration to identify Spanish-speaking people, and "Latino," which focuses on people from Latin America, have become "race" specific when they are not. There is a growing misconception in the United States that Hispanic/Latino is a "race," or that people who are Mexican, Cuban, Colombian, Salvadoran, or Ecuadorian represent a "race" when in fact, they do not. Latin Americans can be presumed to be white, black, indigenous American, Mestizo, "mixed," and even of Asian descent. It seems to me that when people speak about "race," they are generally referring to skin color and simultaneously, to something more than skin color. This is the legacy of people such as Morton, who developed the "science" of race to suit his own prejudices and in the process, got the actual science completely wrong. I find absolutely striking the obsession of "race" and "miscegenation" (defined as "a mixture of races, *especially* marriage, cohabitation, or sexual intercourse between a white person and a member of another race")[1] because it validates the notion of whiteness as separate and superior to all others. Racial namings are not only very revealing, they are demeaning as well.

In the case of my parents, their relationship developed into an international, bilingual, multiethnic partnership that grew out of their curiosity for the world and their desire to make it a better place. My parents were activists—they were deeply involved in the Civil Rights Movement, and were dedicated to social change. The survival of their marriage was rooted in defying the status quo, which is how they raised my older brother and me.

---

1.   "Miscegenation." Merriam-Webster.com, *Merriam-Webster,* www.merriam-webster.com/dictionary/miscegenation. Accessed January 18, 2019.

My father was white, blond and blue/green-eyed. His eyes changed colors depending on lighting or clothing. My mother is dark-skinned, had nearly black hair, and dark brown eyes. My brother, Nicholas Avelino Enright Alava, born August 9, 1971 in Guayaquil, Ecuador and I have caramel skin, dark brown (now greying) hair, and dark brown, nearly black, eyes. Our features resemble those of both of our parents, unsurprisingly, though my brother does possess more of our father's facial features and I, our mother's.

My parents knew their children would face adversity in the United States, and they were proactive in discussing our complex identities with us. They never shielded us from how people might interact with our family, and always emphasized that our strength lay in our complexity. They were proud that we hailed from nearly every continent, that we were native speakers of English and Spanish, and that we lived between the United States and Ecuador. They never allowed external reactions to define their sense of self, and they passed that on to both of us.

My parents chose to raise us in New York City (Brooklyn and the Bronx), a fine choice considering how international and multilingual it is. Nevertheless, when traveling to different parts of the country, heads often turned to gawk at my family. We were stared at as a family of four, but the stares were even more penetrating in disbelief when it was just my father with my brother and me.

For instance, I have very clear memories of my father coming over to me at the park to tell me it was time to go, and children voicing their surprise.

"That's your dad?!"

"Yup!"

"Your real dad?!"

My eyes would narrow into slits and I would respond in a clipped tone. "Of course he's my real dad. Why?"

My wide-eyed interrogators' mouths would form a perfect 'O.' "But he's white!"

I would angrily respond, "So? He's still my dad. I'm mixed. My mom is from Ecuador."

My interrogators would still be aghast despite an explanation I should not have had to give. A pregnant pause would inevitably follow. Then they would say something like, "O-h-kay. I just didn't think that would be your dad."

"Well, he is."

It never ceases to amaze me how freely people felt the need to question the "validity" of our relationship (as if adoption were in fact an invalidation of the parent/child relationship – it is not). We, especially my brother, were so clearly our father's biological children, with the main difference being in the coloring of our skin, but it was clear that people were incapable of seeing past that difference.

I clearly remember coming to my parents upset or angry with yet another anecdote about a question vis-à-vis my identity.

"Mommy? Daddy?"

"Yes?"

"Today someone asked me again if Daddy is my real father. It makes me so angry!"

"You should feel angry, Naomi, and you have every right to feel angry. Remember that you also have every right not to give an answer if you don't want to. But if you do decide to answer, remember to just state the facts and not let the question or the person asking you make you feel bad about yourself or about your family. You are who you are meant to be and when people ask you those questions it says more about their own life experience than it does about you. You owe no one an explanation for who you are."

When my parents discussed these moments with my brother and me they always emphasized that the questions were reflective of the interrogator, not of who we are intrinsically. This was a crucial distinction to make as we were forming our sense of self in a society that in many ways could and would dilute us.

Being asked "Is that your real Dad?" is not an innocent question. It may seem innocent, especially if asked by a young child, but the question carries with it the lessons our society imparts about skin color as definer. This society has categorized people by skin color for generations, so a family like mine, who defies the assumption of skin color as both definer and affinity, unsettles people in many ways. My parents were aware of this and in discussing the wide-eyed, mouths-agape stares with us, would always tell us that we did not need to explain or justify who we are to anyone.

Their approach to discussing these intrusive, hurtful and insulting encounters with us was empowering. From an early age, I knew who I was, and I was unafraid to let people know just that. I knew I should not have to defend who I am or who my family is, and I also knew we must never assume we know who people are or what their relationship is to each other simply by looking at them.

When I would encounter disbelief or aggression growing up, I would always feel comfortable bringing the issue to my parents because they were always thoughtful and supportive in their responses to me. They never silenced me or made me feel that I was overreacting. They listened to me, they believed me, and through that, they empowered me.

As a little girl, other children would taunt me with the insult, "monkey lips." I would often come home crying or angry, and questioned whether or not I did in fact have "monkey lips." My parents would tell me that my thick, full lips were a gift from my African ancestors. They would tell me that when kids called me "monkey lips" they were revealing this society's disdain for features and coloring that clearly hark back to Africa. My parents would tell me that the kids who said such things to me had no understanding of what lay behind their insult, and that it was important that I understand this and not let their words seep into my sense of self. When they said this to me, I would calm down and more importantly, remember what they had told me when kids insulted me.

"Monkey lips" was in fact a racial slur, and even at the tender age of seven or eight, I would tell kids when they called me this that they were being racist, and that my lips were beautiful and a gift from my African ancestors. My response often stunned and silenced them. The teasing would subside, and instead of internalizing the notion that my thick, full lips were ugly, I felt emboldened and proud.

In the fourth grade, when I was about nine-years-old, I took my beloved black cabbage patch doll, Betsy, to school. I was so proud to show her off and at recess was happily sharing her with playmates. At some point, a classmate came up to me and said, "That cabbage patch doll is ugly." Everyone was stunned, staring at me and her to see how I would react. I was furious. This girl had just insulted my beloved doll, which might as well have been my child as far as I was concerned. After glaring her down for a few minutes, I said, "She is not ugly. All cabbage patch dolls look alike. You only think she's ugly because she's black. You're ugly." And then I hit her with the doll. I got in trouble, of course, being sent inside for the rest of recess. Although I am not proud that I hit my classmate, I am proud that I understood precisely what had led her to think Betsy was ugly.

It is true that all cabbage patch dolls look alike, but this society places value on lighter skin, hair and eyes. This classmate saw the doll's dark skin, and immediately decided it was ugly. At the tender age of nine, I understood this, but more importantly,

I understood it to be wrong. There is absolutely nothing inherently better about lighter skin, hair or eyes. My parents knew this, and they were insistent upon imparting this same awareness to their children.

When people asked me if my father was my "real" dad, I knew it was because of the difference in our coloring, and I would turn the very same question back on my interrogators, who would always be momentarily jarred. "Of course. Why?" And I would say, "Why did you ask me? Of course that's my dad," and the discussion would end there. I was very aware of what lay beneath the "innocent" question, and my response illustrated how the approach my parents took in discussing these moments with us, affirmed me.

My parents also knew that the negative reactions people would have about them as a couple were not in fact about them, but rather about our society's racist history. This understanding did not in any way erase their pain or anger, but it did enable them to live their lives and raise their children with armor. Their awareness was their armor. And they passed that same armor onto my brother and me.

It was undoubtedly painful and enervating to feel under constant scrutiny, but as a result of my parents' approach to childrearing, my chi was awake. "Chi," from Chinua Achebe's *Things Fall Apart* meaning "god, guardian angel, personal spirit, soul or spirit-double in Igbo." (Achebe, 1958, 16) Chi in Eastern medicine also refers to one's energy, or life force. My chi has been awoken ever since. ❀

TWO

Speak English. We're in America.

HAVING MY CHI CONSTANTLY AWAKE is exhausting, but it is also an asset. I am attuned to nearly all that is going on around me and am able to respond immediately. I have always been able to think on my feet when confronted with disbelief or aggression. For as long as I could remember, I have been able to tell the difference between genuine interest in my family's complexity and disapproval or judgment about it. I am not saying that I am always right (I am in no one's head but my own), but when your very existence is questioned, you develop defenses. It's almost as if I have grown eyes in the back of my head. I pick up on what has been said, and on what has been left unsaid, in both positive and negative ways.

One particular memory stands out. I had a number of friends in high school who were also bilingual (English/Spanish), and we would sometimes speak to each other in Spanish. It felt like we were in our own little cocoon—a tie that bonded us. I have always felt a sense of home when hearing or speaking

Spanish, so to have friends I could communicate with in Spanish made me feel very much at ease. I could engage with my whole self in these interactions as language informs so much of our identity.

When I was about sixteen years old, I was in art class speaking Spanish with my friends when a classmate, out of the blue, harshly said to me, "Speak English, Naomi. We're in America."

Initially I was stunned into silence, but then I quickly became incensed at her audacity.

Who was she to tell me what language to speak? Or to remind me (as if I needed reminding) of where I am?

Despite my initial reaction, I knew there was so much more behind her statement. My response then, after my momentary silence, was to taunt her with a song and dance rendition of *West Side Story's* "America":

> "I like to be in America!
> O.K. by me in America!
> Everything free in America
> For a small fee in America!"

(Bernstein, Sondheim, 1961)

She and my classmates were astonished at my performance because my tone and face revealed my fury. Having enjoyed watching her squirm with anxiety and confusion, I said, "Who are you to tell me what language to speak? I am bilingual, and I will speak English or Spanish wherever and whenever I please. And isn't your mother Hungarian? Don't you speak Hungarian at home? Why is it okay for you to speak Hungarian but not for me to speak Spanish?"

She became surprised and silent at my response, looking nervously around the room at our classmates. I remember being aware of how my reaction had affected her, and proud because it reflected my understanding that behind her snide comment was the racist belief that as the daughter of Europeans, she was entitled to lay claim over how I, a brown person, should behave and communicate with others.

Who decides who is an American? Why should I, as an English/Spanish speaker, curtail my identity to please or convenience others? In that moment, my parents' approach to always speak openly with me about my identity and our society and its history, served me well. If they had not raised me that way, I would have internalized my classmate's snide, hateful and racist remark instead. I could have questioned the validity of my mother's tongue and spoken less Spanish outside of my home. I would have never questioned what weight her being white and the daughter of European immigrants had in why she thought it was acceptable for her to be bilingual and embrace her culture, but it was not acceptable for me to do the same.

My confidence and outspokenness have always taken people aback because as a brown woman, I am not supposed to feel secure and empowered in my own skin and body. That strong sense of self and belonging, in this society, is supposedly reserved for "those Americans who believe that they are white." (Coates, 2015, 6)

Black and brown people in this society, particularly black and brown women, are supposed to know their place, which is due to our racist and misogynistic history. My classmate had no idea what was coming when she made that remark to me, but for the rest of our high school career together, she never again tried to tell me what language I should speak, or how I should comport myself.

I doubt she could ever understand the profundity of how offensive her remark was, nor do I think I necessarily taught her anything. What is important is that in that moment, I proved to myself I have the tools to understand what such interactions reveal about our society, and that I have the inner strength to defend myself. Others may not be able to see or affirm who I am, but I can, and I always will.

Fast forward to years later and even now when I speak Spanish in public, every once in a while, I am invariably met with hostility, as if I am from another planet. I do not see that happening when I see people speaking French or German. Why does this still happen? It's because the lie continues, that is, America is "white" and in order to be "great," brown-skinned people and in particular, those who speak Spanish should only speak English. It is a lie that has been perpetuated ever since the Pilgrims were exiled from England and arrived here, and even now, we witness our country being led by a racist and xenophobic administration. This ideology has become so ingrained in our national development that we have all accepted it as the default even though it is a fabrication.

Recently, we have witnessed Latin Americans belittled and harassed for speaking Spanish in public. There was the lawyer Aaron Schlossberg, who ironically owns a New York City firm that offers services in Spanish, verbally attack a Fresh Kitchen employee for addressing customers in Spanish. He threatened to call Immigration and Customs Enforcement (ICE) without knowing the person's status and said that if Spanish speakers are going to drain resources, "the least they can do is speak English." (Orjoux, Murphy, Sanchez, 2018) Or how about a Border Patrol agent, who held two women in Havre, Montana for nearly 45 minutes after he overheard them chatting in Spanish in a grocery store – which, he said, "is very unheard of up here." (Wang, 2018) The two incidents illustrate and reinforce that in the United States, people can be targeted for simply communicating in Spanish.

It bewilders me why so many people in this country are intimidated by Latin Americans. But we are dyed into the wool of this country. We have always been here, and we are not going anywhere. Simply put, many of us refuse to abandon our heritage and our language because we do not believe in limiting our abilities. Regardless of the work we dedicate ourselves to, we are keeping the American Dream alive. The question now is, will America be able to confront its fears and prejudices? Time will tell as a country full of possibilities awaits a response. ❈

THREE

Welcome to ADELANTE!

Growing up in New York City, I experienced ethnic and linguistic diversity as the norm, in part because of my own family, but also because my parents ensured that my school and social environments reflected difference. It is somewhat impossible to surround yourself with people just like you when you belong to a family like mine. I used to joke that if I wanted to hang out with only people who were like me culturally, that would limit me to hanging out with my brother. He's great company, to be sure, but one needs a wider circle of people to engage with. In New York City, the minute I left the house, I was exposed to other languages, other cultures and other worldviews.

The high school I attended, Little Red Schoolhouse and Elisabeth Irwin High School, was ethnically and linguistically diverse. My close group of friends included an Ecuadorian-Jew, two Ecuadorian women, a white-black woman, a Guyanese woman, and a Thai-Dutch woman. We in fact dubbed ourselves the "Ethnic Crew" because of how culturally diverse we were. I loved being a part of that circle, and I loved being exposed to multiple cultures right in my hometown. New York City was a special place to grow up in.

Given all of this, when I decided to apply for Early Decision, and chose to attend upon my acceptance, Kenyon College in Gambier, Ohio, my family and friends were shocked. They knew how much I loved growing up and living in New York, as well as my passion for examining issues of racism and identity, so they were concerned when I decided to attend an overwhelmingly homogeneous college. More than once, they asked me if I was sure, and if perhaps I should reevaluate my decision. Ever stubborn, I thanked them for their concern and held firm in my decision to attend Kenyon College. It was where I wanted to go.

Kenyon College's main attraction was their renowned English program and that they did not have a math requirement, an added plus since I had struggled with math throughout my entire life. At the time, I thought I would be an English major, but I ended up becoming an anthropology major instead. Truth be told, the best year of college for me was my junior year studying abroad in Spain. Nevertheless, I do not have any regrets about attending Kenyon College. The classes were excellent, I had amazing professors, and I never would have decided on anthropology as a major or studied abroad had I not gone to Kenyon.

Ultimately, though, the concerns my family and friends expressed about my being one of the few brown students on campus would prove to be a defining measure of my experience at Kenyon. As a freshman, I attended the first meeting of ADELANTE, the Hispanic/Latino Student Organization. Having already noticed how few African American, Latin American, Asian American or Middle Eastern American students there were, I was excited to connect with other Latin Americans on campus. When I received the letter about the organization over the summer, I liked the name, because when translated, the word *"adelante"* means "ahead, forward or onward," but when I read the rest of the letter, I discovered that ADELANTE had been made into an acronym meaning *"Asociación de Estudiantes Latino Americanos de Naciones Tropicales y Exóticas."* This translates to "The Association of Latin American Students from Tropical and Exotic Nations." I was not pleased and I needed clarification from the group as to why they would refer to our cultural heritage as "tropical" and "exotic." I decided this was something worth discussing at my first meeting.

When I arrived at the meeting, after initial introductions, I nervously but determinedly raised my concerns about the acronym. I shared with the group that the word ADELANTE on its own is excellent, but the acronym seemed to defy the positive message of the word as well as perpetuate stereotypes about Latin America. I distinctly remember some classmates at the meeting exchanging looks with each other as I spoke, with some of them responding with a variation of, "What? What do you mean? It's a great word and acronym. It illustrates our love for Latin American cultures." Other classmates did not speak but looked at me with a mixture of blank stares (as if the idea had never occurred to anyone else), or shock (as if there was no way the acronym could be offensive). I was taken aback by the utter confusion my concern was met with. I responded, "But the acronym doesn't in fact illustrate a love for Latin American cultures. What it does is perpetuate stereotypes about the Spanish-speaking world. Tropical and exotic nations? These are not words Latin Americans would use to describe themselves or how they wish to be described."

There was no further examination about my concerns, they simply exchanged nervous and somewhat irritated glances, and in essence told me there was never any intent to insult anyone. I already understood that there was never any wish to offend actual Latin Americans, but the name represents what is known in equity circles as "intent versus impact." Their *intent* may not have been to demean or stereotype, but the *impact* of their actions led to feeling demeaned and stereotyped. In the end, there was no desire on their part to reconsider the ADELANTE acronym. I was frustrated and disappointed to say the least, and that ended up being the first and last "Hispanic/Latino Student Organization" meeting I attended in college.

I realized in that brief but profound exchange that the organization aimed to serve the interests of white students, who had very little understanding of Latin American identities or of Latin America/the Caribbean. The "Hispanic/Latino Student Organization" then was not in fact about Latin Americans at all.

This experience also solidified for me just how much of an outsider I can be and how complex examining issues of identity is. I was disheartened to learn that the one organization on campus that was ostensibly set up to serve Latin Americans, was in fact a space for white students to explore their "interest" in Latin America and the Caribbean, which sadly did not seem to extend to its people.

The interests expressed in that first (and last) meeting were for food, music, textiles, and travel. My classmates brought up ideas for what to do for "Hispanic Heritage Month" (September 15-October 15) and all of their ideas revolved around the themes I mentioned above. I remember statements like, "We should make empanadas!," or "We should have a salsa class!," or "Maybe we could have a workshop on how to make traditional Guatemalan clothing?" and lastly, "Maybe we could have, like, a mini trip around different parts of Latin America? So people could feel like they've actually been to the region!"

These interests have their merit – I do not mean to discredit or dismiss them – but they do not translate to what a "Hispanic/Latino Student Organization" should be. In fact, these interests perpetuate the "othering" of blackness and brownness, and the "normalizing" of whiteness. I have had more than one experience when, after a white person discovers I speak Spanish, they ask me to "say something." It has always irritated and offended me as it makes my mother tongue seem like it exists to serve someone else's curiosity or fascination. Spanish is a tool for communication in many countries throughout the world.

My experience with ADELANTE at Kenyon College highlighted for me how deep racism really is in our country. When I look back on how I handled that ADELANTE meeting, though, I feel I should not have been so dismissive and created a chance for true dialogue. Our brief exchange was not enough to get at the heart of my concerns that could have prompted change. I was only eighteen years old, however, and completely out of my element, so I did what came natural to me – in order to protect myself, I walked away. But the experience did teach me a great deal about how society's handling of racism and cultural difference are so often superficial, how we do not deal with history, and how that history plays out in the present.

Those white students who thought an acronym that translates Hispanic/Latino cultures as "tropical" and "exotic" is proof of this. Those classmates' intentions were informed by the lessons they had absorbed their entire lives about whiteness as the "norm." They "simply were," whereas the entire diversity of Spanish-speaking countries became "the other" and a source of curiosity.

My understanding of the significance of that experience helped benefit my examination of racism and identity. My family and friends were right that Kenyon College was culturally dissimilar from me, and that I would feel out of place. But had I not attended Kenyon College, I would have perhaps not been forced to face these historical and societal truths.

I went to college assuming most people grew up exposed to differences of all kinds, but my time there proved me wrong. I was provincial in my own way and though there were some painful and infuriating moments like my attendance at the AD-ELANTE meeting, I was forced to take stock of my own worldview and reexamine how to challenge racism and highlight the complexity of identity. ✿

Sevilla

DURING MY JUNIOR YEAR OF COLLEGE, I had the privilege to study and live in Sevilla, Spain. I chose Sevilla both because it was not Latin America (I had grown up going to visit my maternal family in Ecuador), and because I had never lived completely immersed in Spanish.

In high school, I studied French but when I arrived at Kenyon College, I decided to study Spanish. I had been raised speaking both English and Spanish seamlessly, and my mother would make me read and write in Spanish, mainly through correspondence with my relatives, but I had never studied it formally. Throughout my childhood and adolescence, I would sometimes spend six weeks at a time visiting my family in Ecuador. Being fully immersed in Spanish during those visits was central to my bilingualism, which comforted the layers of my identity. I remember when I would first arrive during those visits, I would falter some when speaking Spanish, primarily because outside of my home, my world was dominated by

English. But by the end of those visits, I would sound like a local Ecuadorian, in pronunciation and in the colloquialisms I would use. It would always make my mother beam when we would get off the plane sounding so Ecuadorian. Those extended visits with my family in Ecuador would cement my sense of self as a native English and Spanish speaker as well as an American and an Ecuadorian.

Given that I had never formally studied my maternal tongue, however, I decided in college that it was time to do so. As a result of my fluency, as a freshman I was placed in a literature course for juniors and seniors. I was both proud and intimidated. I did well, though, and as my reading and writing in Spanish improved, I decided it would benefit me even further to immerse myself completely in the language. Thus, I made the decision to study abroad in Sevilla, Spain my junior year.

I went to Sevilla with a whole host of preconceived notions about what I would experience and how I would be viewed or treated given that I am Latina. Although I observed rampant racism, particularly anti-Moroccan in Sevilla, I was shocked to discover not only how comfortable I felt but how welcoming Sevillanos were to me. I lived with a local family my first two and a half months in Sevilla, and my host mother told me I could easily pass for a Sevillana. Of all the places I would have thought to "blend in," Spain was not one of them. It was a lesson to me in terms of my own assumptions and prejudice.

Nevertheless, the colonial history between Spain and Latin America never escaped my attention, and the anti-Moroccan racism was particularly present. When I traveled to Morocco with a friend and a group of Sevillanos, I observed how more than one Sevillano made fun of the language, the food, the clothing while we were there. It angered me, particularly because Moors ruled Spain for 800 years, so the Spanish language, architecture and food are all descendants of Moorish culture.

The word *"ojalá"* (god willing), for example, descends from the Arabic *("inshaallah")*. My physical appearance, which resembles Sevillanos, is also related to the history of Moorish rule, proving it is the direct result of the genetic mixture responsible for the darker physical appearance of Southern Spaniards. My looking like a Sevillana comes from that mixture as well as from the Semitic blood I inherited from my father. All of these truths were on my mind as I traveled through Morocco, and I learned a great deal from the experience.

Despite my observations from that specific trip, over the course of the nine months I lived in Sevilla, I personally felt welcome. I had sincerely never experienced such comfort. To simply "be" had never, until living in Sevilla, existed for me. Growing up I had come to peace with standing apart from Americans as well as from Ecuadorians, but when I arrived in Sevilla and found not only that I physically resembled the locals, but the language, food and music all felt familiar to me, I realized how much I had been yearning to simply "be."

I have no doubt that my comfort in Sevilla was due in large part to my being a Spanish speaker. Although my accent and vocabulary differed from that of Sevillanos, it is the same language, and throughout my time in Sevilla I began to contemplate the link between language and identity. I had never given my bilingualism much thought. It was simply the norm for me – some people speak one language and some people speak more than one language.

Living in Sevilla, however, it began to dawn on me just how much my being bilingual had informed my self-concept and worldview. There is an aspect of the Spanish language that I have always preferred. It is my mother tongue, so in some ways it is the language of respite for me. When I hear Spanish, I feel instantly more relaxed. I am certain my body and brain remember being lulled to sleep in Spanish. Growing up having visited family in Ecuador and being immersed in the Spanish language always provided a sense of solace for me. I remember walking in my mother's neighborhood in Guayaquil, and feeling literally connected to the earth. It felt as if the air and ground recognized me. I would, even at the tender age of thirteen, think of how my ancestors had breathed and walked the same terrain, and that some part of me was meant to be here.

At the Universidad de Sevilla one morning I asked for *"café con leche."* When I placed the cup to my lips, I was instantly transported to my Abuelita's (maternal grandmother's) dining room table at age four in 1982 in Guayaquil. Tasting that coffee, which in Sevilla is called *"leche manchada"* (stained milk), my grandmother was brought back to me, even if only for a moment, and more importantly, I felt a sense of home, comfort and calm.

Sevilla is in Southern Spain, so the weather is quite sunny and warm. The sun and sky itself would often remind me of Guayaquil. As I walked around the city, details like how the trees were painted white about one-third of the way up, transported me instantly to Guayaquil. The cobblestone streets, the small, family-owned shops, the gates around small stores where one might buy gum or candy, the colors of the homes, the design of the parks, hearing people call me *"niña"* (girl), or how they greet each other, saying, *"Buenas,"* which is shorthand for good morning, afternoon or evening. It was all so familiar to me.

As I walked around the city and became friendly with local shopkeepers and neighbors, I realized just how much being a Spanish speaker not only meant to me, but how much it had informed who I am. My Spanish over the course of those nine months improved tremendously. Using it day in and day out, in every context possible, improved my language skills as well as my confidence.

I have a clear memory of having to go to Citibank to deal with some issues with taking money out of my account while abroad. As I waited my turn, I felt my stomach twist with anxiety, unsure whether or not I would be able to handle this business transaction entirely in Spanish. A friend of mine was with me for moral support. When my turn came, I found to my surprise and delight that I was able to communicate seamlessly. All the vocabulary I needed for that specific interaction was at my fingertips, and I remember the teller being surprised to hear how fluent I was. I resolved the issue and as I walked out, with my head held high rather than with my stomach tied in knots, my friend said to me, "Wow! You really do speak Spanish!"

Every aspect of living in Sevilla reinforced for me how much I love the Spanish language and the customs attached to it. For me, Spanish speakers are warm and friendly when they interact with one another. It is a formal language and I believe that formality results in gentler interactions. Spanish is, in my mind, much more lyrical than the English language.

After being in Sevilla I also understood that none of us would be who we are without the language, or languages, that we speak. ✹

FIVE

Language, Culture and Identity

WHEN I GRADUATED FROM Kenyon College in May 2000, I had a few different jobs, including Project Assistant for the LGBT & AIDS Rights Project at the American Civil Liberties Union (ACLU). I worked at the ACLU thinking I might become a Social Justice Lawyer. After miserably failing the LSAT, however, I decided law was not the path for me. I worked at the ACLU from 2001 to 2004. When I left in 2004, I took some time to contemplate my professional future while visiting family in Ecuador.

A few weeks into my stay in Ecuador, my parents arrived. I vividly remember discussing my professional future with my father one day when he jokingly said, "Have you ever considered joining the family business?" I chuckled and said, "What family business? We don't own any businesses." He wisely responded, "Teaching." I smiled because in some ways, his description of it as a "family business" was extremely apt. I am a descendant of educators. My maternal grandmother was a teacher – she stopped teaching after becoming a mother, and both of my parents were educators. My father was an administrator for years at Lehman College in the Bronx, and my mother had taught for years, ending her teaching career as an English teacher and Dean at Horace Mann School, also in the Bronx. I sincerely never considered teaching until that conversation with my father.

Soon after returning to the States in January 2005, I began substitute teaching at Riverdale Country School in the Bronx. I filled in for a number of teachers covering an assortment of subjects and grades, and I found I had a knack for the classroom. I was able to connect easily with students of all ages, and I had a nice balance of tough love and humor. I took delight in having command of the classroom and I relished seeing students' faces light up when they discovered something new. As I taught, I really enjoyed teaching in the Spanish language classroom. Similarly to my experience in Sevilla, I loved engaging with both of my native languages. The students would in fact comment on how I changed depending on the language I was speaking–they would tell me my voice was softer and calmer in Spanish.

In the spring of 2005, I was able to fill an assistant first grade teacher position at the Fieldston School in the Bronx. It was a rare opportunity to obtain a full time position so late in the school year. My time there, though, improved my skills in the classroom and solidified my desire to become a teacher. I did realize, however, that I preferred teaching Spanish to being a grade-level teacher, so I applied for a position to teach fifth grade Spanish at Riverdale Country School (RCS) for the 2005-2006 school year. The job also required teaching as an assistant teacher in a first grade classroom, but the Spanish portion I knew would be invaluable. I was offered that position and became a Spanish teacher in September 2005.

I thoroughly loved teaching that fifth grade Spanish class–and began searching for a full-time Spanish teaching position. In my role as a fifth grade Spanish teacher, I began to devise my own curriculum, which emphasized what I had come to understand in Sevilla – the connection between language, culture and identity.

My students very much appreciated this, particularly my bilingual/multilingual students, and especially those whose families recently immigrated to the United States. As I would speak to these points, the faces of those students who were exposed to multiple languages and/or cultures would light up. They would smile broadly and make statements like:

> "That's so true! My mom is Japanese, and I can never explain Japanese jokes to my American friends. They just wouldn't get it. It just doesn't translate the same." or,

> "Yeah, when I'm in the Dominican Republic with my family, I always feel more peaceful. It's like even just having Spanish all around me makes me feel better."

Like me in Sevilla, those students were able to engage with their whole selves in my classroom.

In my job search, I applied to a fifth to eighth grade Spanish teaching position at Manhattan Country School (MCS), which at the time was located on the Upper East Side of Manhattan. MCS is a uniquely independent school. It was founded in 1966, born out of the Civil Rights Movement, by Gus and Marty Trowbridge, who felt that socioeconomic and ethnic diversity were crucial to a child's learning environment as well as to his or her's growth as an individual and as a global citizen. MCS, from its inception, has had sliding scale tuition and during its entire existence has been able to maintain a student population with no socioeconomic or ethnic majority. I was thrilled they offered me a position, even more so after reading Gus Trowbridge's memoir about his life and the founding of MCS, *Begin with a Dream: How a Private School with a Public Mission Changed the Politics of Race, Class and Gender in American Education* (2005).

Given MCS's mission and history, as well as my own passion and history, we agreed that in addition to learning the mechanics of the Spanish language, it was crucial that my students also study the cultures and identities that exist within the Spanish-speaking world. As I had done at Riverdale Country School, I wished for my students at MCS to engage with the inextricable link that exists between language, culture and identity. I dove into my role at MCS, excited for the freedom to devise my own curricula and for all that my students would learn.

I would often begin the school year asking my students to define language and culture, and throughout the year would engage them in reflections about the power of language and how it informs who we are and how we see the world. I had my students reflect on these questions in age-appropriate ways but also devised long-term projects with these questions in mind.

My fifth graders would write personal essays using the verb *"ser"* (to be). My sixth graders would do a small group study of a Spanish-speaking country and present upon the history, languages, and other cultural aspects of their specific country. My seventh graders would write *"Soy De"* ("I Am From") poems and my eighth graders would work on projects related to current events. For example, one year I had my eighth graders work on a project focused on immigration entitled *"Todos Somos Inmigrantes"* ("We Are All Immigrants").

I loved all of the projects I would have my students engage in, but the seventh grade *"Soy De"* ("I Am From") poems were by far my favorite. The prose my students would write was phenomenal and illustrated how introspective and insightful children are about their identities.

One year, a student who was half-Cuban American wrote a poem including these lines:

> *"Soy del país prohibido. La bandera lavada con lágrimas. Pero aún seca con las sonrisas de la isla. Secándose en la belleza tropical. Soy del país prohibido. La gente débil. La isla fuerte. Yo soy Cuba."*

("I am from the forbidden country. The flag washed with tears. Yet dried with the smiles of the island. Drying in the tropical beauty. I am from the forbidden country. The people weak. The island strong. I am Cuba.")

That same year another student wrote:

> *"Yo soy el universo, yo soy un grano de arena. Soy todo, yo soy uno. Yo soy la verdad, yo soy la mentira. Soy todo y soy nada. Yo soy una mota de polvo en este mundo que todavía no he visto. Soy la risa, soy la alegría. Yo soy la tristeza, yo soy lágrimas. Yo soy el amor, yo soy el odio."*

("I am the universe, I am a grain of sand. I am all, I am one. I am truth, I am lies. I am everything and I am nothing. I am a speck of dust in this world I have not yet seen. I am laughter, I am joy. I am sadness, I am tears. I am love, I am hatred.")

As I had observed at RCS, while my discussions would often resonate most with my bilingual/multilingual students, they informed my monolingual students as well. It was a chance for my bilingual/multilingual students to embrace the multiplicity of their identities—from their perspective being informed by their code switching to a shift in their tone of voice depending on the language they were speaking—as well as a chance for my monolingual students to reflect on how speaking one language also informed their self-concept and worldview. I had a student once write to me, "I want to thank you for being a great teacher. In Spanish class for the past two years, you have been pushing my thinking of language. You have made it easier for me to learn other languages as well as help me with everyday communication."

That particular student had absorbed all I had set out to do as a Spanish teacher. He had understood the inextricable link that exists between language, culture and identity. Through the process of examining these links my students and I often discussed larger historical and systemic issues.

As a result of my classes I offered more than one elective, which afforded me the chance to examine certain issues more deeply. I offered a Spanish language film elective where we watched films such as *El Norte* (1983), *La Historia Oficial* (1985), *Stand and Deliver* (1988) and *Sugar* (2008), discussing (respectively) indigenous identity and illegal immigration, the Dirty War and *"los desaparecidos,"* educational inequity and the cost of immigrating to the U.S. for economic opportunity. These films introduced my students not only to a wide range of Spanish accents and vocabulary, but also to a wide range of issues that have affected the Spanish-speaking world.

My students experienced history and realities in my film elective that they may have otherwise not been exposed to. *Stand and Deliver* was one film that seemed to especially affect my students, since Manhattan Country School students have always been taught to speak up against inequity. The fact that it was based on a true story upset them quite a bit. When we discussed the film, they would make comments such as, "It's so obvious that it was racism. If those students had been white at an elite school and had all done well on the calculus exam, no one would have questioned it. They would have been celebrated. But since they were poor and mostly Latino, the assumption was that of course they'd cheated. That's so wrong." Their understanding of the systemic issues was impressive and as a teacher, it was exciting to see all that they understood and the armor their understanding gave them in the world.

One year, I offered an elective unrelated to my Spanish teaching entitled "Beyond Race." In this elective my students read and discussed Peggy McIntosh's 1989 article "White Privilege: Unpacking the Invisible Knapsack" as well as watched and discussed episodes of Dr. Henry Louis Gates Jr.'s PBS program, *Finding Your Roots,* a documentary television series that uses traditional genealogical research and genetics to discover the family history of well-known Americans. We would discuss the history and perpetuation of systemic racism and the nuance of identity. My students were particularly floored by the construction of racial difference and whiteness. I remember one student (an eighth grader) saying, "That is so crazy to think that an idea created a whole system of giving power to white people. And we still believe that idea!" He could not have been more right. In those moments, the power I held as an educator was palpable and I began to yearn to engage with these issues with students more often and more directly.

With this desire in mind, in another year, I had my seventh and eighth grade students engage in The Race Card Project—an online project created by Michelle Norris, former host at NPR—in which participants are asked to write six-word essays about racism and identity. The responses from my students were incredible. Among them were:

"My family is not an experiment."

"Racism is like a sixth sense."

"So now it's always the white?" and

"Why me? A black man's motto."

It was powerful to see what had occurred to these thirteen and fourteen-year-old students, and to engage them in honest dialogue about their responses. The discussion was not easy as their six-word essays revealed a wide range of personal experiences, but the opportunity to engage with each other was invaluable and further motivated me to have my students think critically about identity.

Through my students' learning, in my Spanish classroom as well as in my electives, I was able to see firsthand how examining identity closely, with an understanding of its layers, illuminates everyone's complexity and allows for true dialogue and change. ✱

Swimming Against the Tide

O N MARCH 17, 2006, at a bar called Match.com, I met my future husband, Adam Whittaker. My husband was born March 1979 in Louisville, Kentucky. He has one older brother and lived in Jeffersonville, Indiana until age five, when he and his family moved to Cincinnati, Ohio. Adam is white, of Western European (mainly Irish and German) ancestry and is monolingual.

On his maternal side, Adam has family who were dedicated abolitionists. One family member, Charles Beggs, for whom Charlestown, Indiana was named, was a key player in not allowing Indiana to become a slave state, and his maternal grandfather hired black men to work with him. At his grandfather's funeral in October 1988, a black man came up to my mother-in-law to tell her had it not been for her father hiring him, he would have been unable to work. That tribute speaks to the value system in Adam's family history and to who he is as a result. I was both proud and impressed when I heard these anecdotes from his maternal history.

On his paternal side, Adam's dad was the first in his nuclear family to attend college. He was a stay-at-home father for a time when Adam and his brother were young. Adam has always told me of the connection between seeing his mother work outside of the home and his father stay at home with his feminism. My in-laws never took issue with Adam and me as a multiethnic couple and in fact have, like Adam, always made me feel that my complexity simply enhances who I am.

Adam studied Communications Design at Pratt University in Brooklyn, graduating in May 2001, and has made a career as a Creative Director. Since I attended Kenyon, I have always teased Adam that when I went to his home state for college, I knew to return to my own and that when he went to my hometown for college, he knew to stay.

On the surface, it would seem that Adam and I have little in common, but truth be told, he always makes me feel seen and heard, and he makes me laugh like none other. He has olive-green eyes, quite striking, and once early on in our relationship he said, *"¡Tengo aceitunas en los ojos!"* which literally translates to "I have olives in my eyes!" It was very witty, and spoke to his desire to engage with my maternal tongue.

Adam is open-minded, kind, generous, observant, sensitive and aware. From the moment we met, I have spoken with him openly about my multiethnic, bilingual identity and rather than behave as if my complexity made me an oddity, he has always respected and accepted me as I am. I felt at home with Adam and soon after we met, fell in love with him.

In some ways, Adam reminded me of my father in that despite his privilege as a heterosexual, white, male, he has always felt outraged by racism and injustice of any kind. Adam has always been interested in people and has never struggled with seeing everyone's full humanity.

One of the most horrible consequences of an ideology of racial difference and whiteness and their results, systemic racism and white supremacy, is that they strip black and brown people of their humanity and allow white people to not see themselves in black and brown people. If systemic racism and white supremacy are viewed as the inevitable result of white people's "inherent superiority," then it becomes nearly impossible to combat. With an ideology of racial difference and whiteness, the disenfranchisement, marginalization and criminalization of blackness and brownness is the natural order of things.

Adam early on proved to me that he understood the destructiveness of this history and that he wished to be part of creating positive change. In 2007, when Barack Obama announced his candidacy for the presidency, Adam and I, and our families, were ecstatic. We were all deeply involved in his campaign, canvassing different neighborhoods and making phone calls. We all felt that this was exactly what this country needed and we wished to experience the shift firsthand. Observing my future husband's passion during Obama's campaign filled me with gratitude and love. This was a man after my own heart – an empathic, strong and determined man who fights for what he believes in.

Adam and I became engaged on March 15, 2008 and were married in Manhattan on May 31, 2009. As we had come to know each other and each other's families, I knew I had found my best friend and life partner. Adam has always made me feel at home and his family has always made me feel welcome. In fact when I met my future in-laws, it became clear to me why Adam is who he is. He was raised to be compassionate and compassion is a key ingredient to being a humanitarian and a defender of social justice. Adam and his family openly discuss systemic dominance and oppression and wish to be part of the movement to create true systemic change.

Over the course of our relationship, Adam has illustrated to me time and time again how committed he is to being part of the change he wishes to see. Although he does not speak Spanish, over the years he has learned key phrases and has never interfered with my determination for our son to be bilingual. If he had not agreed to my speaking nearly exclusively to our son in Spanish, our son would not be bilingual. One key Spanish phrase he has learned, *"Buen provecho,"* which we say at the beginning of all meals, he taught to his family as well and now when I am with my in-laws, we all say it. When I insisted upon giving our son a name spelled and pronounced in Spanish, he agreed, understanding that his name would tell part of his story and that having a Spanish name would be an immediate, tangible link to part of his inheritance on my side.

When we were dating, knowing how much I love to read, especially books about language and identity, Adam bought me Junot Díaz's *The Brief Wondrous Life of Oscar Wao* (2007) and in the dedication wrote, "I love everything about you, and I want to remind you of that forever. I thought this book might remind you of your heritage that I love and want to be a part of." When I read that, my heart soared because it became clear to me then that I had met a man who wished to know me as I am, and would never minimize any part of who I am.

The fact that Adam decided to attend college in New York City and stay, also speaks to his open-mindedness and to his desire to be part of a forward-thinking world. His hometown, Mariemont, Ohio, could not be more different from New York City. When we visit, it never ceases to amaze me how little diversity of any kind there is in his hometown. Cincinnati, the city, has plenty of diversity but the surrounding towns are often ethnically homogenous and quite split between the "white" side and the "black" side. Adam told me he had no classmates who were African American, Latin American, Asian American, or Middle Eastern American as a child, and in high school maybe had two classmates who were not white Americans. He told me it never sat well with him, that he had thought it odd, and that he was determined to study and live elsewhere for college. Choosing New York City would alter the course of his life, bringing our paths together, and altering the course of my life as well.

Despite the differences in our upbringing and our family histories, at the core Adam and I share a belief in the collectiveness of humanity and the power of one. He is descended from change agents, as am I, and together, we created and are raising another change agent.

My husband and I have always spoken about the nuance and complexity of identity. In our conversations, I have often shared with Adam the pain I always experience being on the fringe—I am never fully at home anywhere. I will never forget that he once told me in response to one of these conversations that my place is to "swim against the tide." He told me I should "relish" that truth and that he is content to swim against the tide alongside me. ❀

SEVEN

Yes, He Is My Biological Son

WHEN WE BECAME ENGAGED, Adam and I knew that we wanted to have a child. In March 2010, I became pregnant and both of us, and our families anxiously awaited the arrival of our creation. Our child would be the first grandchild on both sides and when I went into labor in late November 2010, both sets of soon-to-be-grandparents were in the hospital with us. At 1:36 pm on December 1, 2010, Adam and I welcomed our son, Sebastián Adam, into the world. I gave birth via C-section so was unable to immediately hold my son, but when Adam brought him over to me, I kissed his face and remember thinking he was absolutely gorgeous. We could not have been more excited to begin our life as a nuclear family of three.

Our son was born with light skin, blond hair and blue-green eyes. When I was pregnant with Sebastián, I thought and talked quite a bit about what he might look like, given his ethnic mixture. I figured he would be on the lighter end, but I will not deny that even I was a bit in shock to see him when he was placed in my arms. I remember searching his face for a sign of me and I found it in his lips. They, like mine, are thick and full, a gift from our African ancestors.

Although it was initially a bit jarring to see just how light-skinned our son was, I was also not surprised. It made sense—Adam is nearly entirely of Western European ancestry and between my father's Eastern European and my mother's Spanish ancestry, I am largely European in my inheritance as well. But because of this country's fixation on skin color, our relationship as mother and son has been challenged from the moment we brought him home from the hospital.

It was not easy to recover from a C-section and adjust to motherhood amidst disbelief. I saw myself in him, as did anyone who looked beyond the surface, but it was clear that our difference in coloring is what seemed to matter most to others.

Since his birth, I have spoken nearly exclusively to my son in Spanish. He is now, at eight years old, completely bilingual. He shocks many when he opens his mouth speaking rapid-fire, flawless Spanish. When he was quite young, around two or three years old, he did not realize that I also spoke English, so he would translate what people had said to me! It was very cute, and evidence that for him, the Spanish language was omnipresent.

And his name is purposeful—it is spelled and pronounced in Spanish so that he and the world knows that he is also Latino. It is a tangible link to his Ecuadorian inheritance, and a crucial aspect of his identity.

Ever since my son was born, I have refused to accept his "whiteness." I believe my son's physical appearance does not tell his story. I also believe my son's physical appearance should not automatically entitle him to a life of protection and privilege. Adam and I are parenting our son in a way that intentionally challenges systemic racism and white supremacy along with the ethos that created both.

Adam has always emphasized the physical similitude Sebastián shares with me as well as with him. He too is teaching Sebastián that skin color does not equate affinity or similitude.

Our refusal to accept our son's "whiteness" speaks to this intentionality. Adam and I know that despite how our son looks and is perceived, his truth is much more nuanced, and that he must know this in order to see the wholeness of both himself and of others. Our son will be better equipped to challenge racism if he understands himself to be more than what the American system tells him he is.

I, as his mother, also refuse to be erased. I carried my son within my own body for forty-one weeks and brought him into the world after two days of labor followed by a C-section. I am a deeply devoted mother, so when we are out in the world and people instantly dismiss me because of our difference in coloring, it stings.

I remember bringing him to a café that I frequented near Manhattan Country School when he was no older than three years old. I introduced him to the employees I always chatted with and one said to me, *"No se te parece nada."* ("He looks nothing like you.") I felt the familiar internal constriction of anger but calmly and factually responded, *"Si sólo miras la superficie."* ("If you only look at the surface.") The employee understood, but what matters more, is that exchanges like that model for my son not only how to respond confidently and proactively but how to provide a counter-narrative.

I am certain that had I not been raised the way I was – to understand our country's history of systemic racism and the ideology that created that system, I would have easily accepted my son's "whiteness," and in fact may have felt grateful for it. But because of my parents' lessons to me about the exterior (our society) being the problem and what needs to change – not me – as well as because of who I married and the values we share – my son knows who he is. ✳

EIGHT

In The Sun

GROWING UP, I WAS CLOSE to both of my parents in different ways, but like many little girls, I was very attached to my father. I share many of my mother's personality traits but in some profound ways, I am much more my father's child. My father was a reader and an observer – he liked to take in the people and the scene around him before he would engage. I am exactly the same. One of my father's mantras in fact was, *"El que lee nunca se aburre."* ("Those who read are never bored.") He could not have ben more right.

As a child, my father and I would take long walks together, discussing anything and everything. We would often discuss family and identity, my deepest passions for as long as I can remember. My father always spoke to me about the complexity of people, how we all have multilayered stories that culminate in the creation of who we are. With my father, I learned to never assume anything.

I remember him saying to me, in response to my complaints about people's dismissal of us as father and daughter, "I know it angers and hurts you, Naomi, but you have to learn not to allow what other people feel or think to dictate how you feel or think. When people dismiss the possibility of me being your father, or of you being my daughter, you need to remember that they might have a whole other family experience and history than you. People don't always dismiss our relationship out of malice. In fact, it is more often than not out of a lack of exposure. I think it would help you to remember that. That way when you respond, you won't shut the other person down. And you will also grow as an individual from these encounters." This is just one example of the profound advice he would give me on our walks that helped me to become a more empathic and broad-minded individual.

I feel very grateful to have come from such a wonderful man and to have married one. When Sebastián was born, my father was overjoyed. He would come to our home nearly every day to be with us, and was central to my healing emotionally from having had to give birth via C-section. Those early days of motherhood walking with my newborn son and my beloved father were very special and are treasured memories.

In January 2011, a month after Sebastián was born, I began to worry that there was something wrong with my father, however. He seemed slightly thinner and frailer to me and I expressed these fears to my family. My family chalked my worries to new motherhood, which I could understand. It is easy to think of the fleetingness of life once one has had a child. Nevertheless, I continued to insist that something was wrong.

As 2011 progressed, my father began to lose more weight at an alarming rate, and in September, he was diagnosed with Stage 4 pancreatic cancer. I will never forget him telling me his diagnosis over the phone as I walked with baby Sebastián into the supermarket. My eyes filled with tears, but I kept my voice steady and said, "We'll fight it, Daddy. Maybe you will be okay." He responded, *"Gracias,* pumpkin. Maybe." But the unspoken truth we all understood is that his diagnosis was a death sentence and that he was not long for this world.

On November 29, 2011, two days before my son's first birthday, I lost my seventy-one-year-old father. The day he died was cloudy and dreary, but upon leaving the hospital, the sun broke through the clouds and I immediately felt his presence. I looked up and said, "That's Papi." I have felt his presence in the sun ever since. Nevertheless, his death deeply traumatized and transformed me. Part of that transformation has to do specifically with racism and identity.

My father in many ways contextualized for others my son's physical appearance. When I would be out in the world with my baby and my father, and explained who we were to each other, people would nod and grasp how and why my son is so light-skinned. Sebastián also inherited my father's eyes – just like his Abo (as we have come to call him in photos), Sebastián's blue-green eyes change depending on the light and his clothing.

After my father died, however, there was no one from my side of the family to contextualize for others that so much of my son's "whiteness" is also inherited from me. People now take one look at my brown face and discard the possibility that I could have brought forth this "white" child. Without my father, I became even more attuned to what lay beneath the assumptions. And I became even more determined to challenge it.

Profound change, of any kind, is traumatic. Becoming a parent is one of life's biggest and most permanent transformations, as is the loss of a parent.

The confluence of my gain and my loss as well as the professional work I had been doing of having students think critically about history and the complexity of identity, dramatically shifted my mindset. I had my own lived history of how people would respond to my family, particularly to my father and me, and now with my son in the world, it was as if I had on 3-D glasses. I could see the difference in the reactions to my father and me versus to my son and me, and all of a sudden, I could see further. ✸

NINE

Is Race Real?

I N SEPTEMBER 2011, nine months after giving birth, I returned to Manhattan Country School as the Upper School Spanish Teacher. Soon after returning, however, I began to notice both that my passion for examining identity outweighed my passion for teaching Spanish and that I felt exhausted by the Spanish teaching given that I spoke exclusively to my son in Spanish. These observations were the beginning of a reevaluation of my professional life.

At the New York State Association of Independent Schools' (NYSAIS) Diversity Conference in April 2013, I engaged in an exercise that solidified my desire to leave the Spanish language classroom. We were all asked to write six-word essays that condensed our experience, thoughts and feelings about racism and identity onto an index card. My statement – "Yes, he is my biological son." – came to me immediately. I then volunteered to share and expand upon it with the entire conference. Despite my shaking legs and beating heart, I felt empowered after my share and realized then that I had to professionally delve more deeply into examining racism, culture, identity and systemic change.

In June 2014, after eight years as a Spanish teacher, I left Manhattan Country School and that August began to work as a Diversity Associate in the Office of Diversity at Horace Mann School in the Bronx. I was thrilled to have found a position that would enable me to devote myself wholly to examining history, systems of subjugation and power, and the complexity of identity. It was also a nice coincidence that I would be working at the school my mother had taught at for ten years, and that I had attended as a seventh and eighth grade student. There was a lot of history there. My mother had in fact been a founding member of the Valuing Difference Committee, which set the stage for the creation of the Office of Diversity.

The work of the Office of Diversity focused on all aspects of identity, but given my own personal history, the work focusing on racism and identity is what spoke to me most. I began to notice, however, a pattern during discussions about racism and identity that discomfited me. More often than not, the language used to discuss racism nearly always solidified the erroneous notion of inherent racial difference.

For example, I would often hear and read statements such as "We know race is a social construct, but race is real," or calling affinity groups "race-based," or "We can't behave as if children don't see race. They do." I began to notice that statements like these not only reinforce race as an immutable concept, but they leave no room for a family like my own, or more specifically, for a child like mine. I also noticed that said statements reinforce the supposed automatic privilege, protection and power of whiteness.

I would often push back with statements such as, "It seems like cognitive dissonance to me to say on the one hand that race is a social construct, but then reinforce it by saying it's real," or "Why aren't affinity groups called 'ethnicity or culture' based as they are groups for people who share an identity but certainly not a race?," or "How is it that children see race exactly? If race is a social construct and has no biological basis then how can we claim to see it?"

My colleagues would listen respectfully, but seemed to feel that this is the language we know, so this is the language we must use. Despite many agreeing with my point about how the language of race in fact corroborates its destructive ideology, there was a sense that there was no way around it.

I remember speaking with two colleagues one day about this and them saying to me, "Naomi, we understand what you mean but if we don't say race, that's just another way of skirting the real issues. Race is the issue and by not naming it, we get ourselves into dangerous territory. Not naming race is the equivalence of colorblindness, which I know you agree is wrong."

To this I responded, "I am absolutely not advocating for colorblindness but race as a concept, as a belief system, is what in fact attaches value to skin color and I think in order to deal with the real issues, it is racism we need to name every time. Not race. Race is part of why systemic racism was created and why it has continued to thrive."

There were many discussions like this—they never necessarily landed in a place of agreement, but they were respectful discussions and they helped me clarify my thinking about how crucial the language we use is in how we challenge systemic racism.

In these exchanges, there also seemed to be a sense that if we dismiss the language of race, we are minimizing the lived reality of systemic racism. This is a fair and genuine concern, one I grapple with too, but the more I realized that the language of race in fact reinforces its ideology of inherent difference, the more determined I felt that as a society, we cannot even begin to think of challenging systemic racism if we accept the foundation that created it.

The foundation of systemic racism is an ideology both of an inherent difference between white people and everyone else (and their lived experiences) as well as of whiteness as shield and protector. Whiteness is at the core of why systemic racism has been able to remain in place, and why it continues to thrive. For far too long, far too many groups of immigrants have been able to adopt whiteness, at the expense of people of color, most specifically, at the expense of black people.

It became clear to me in the work that I was doing, and in the conversations I was having, that no real systemic change will occur in our country if we use the tools that built the system to ostensibly try to dismantle it.

The writer and activist Audre Lorde (2007, 112) once said, "The master's tools will never dismantle the master's house." The language and ideology of racial difference and whiteness are undoubtedly the master's tools. ✻

Naomi Raquel Enright

TEN

I Do Not See Race. I See Racism.

RATHER THAN SAYING, "Race is real," we should be saying, "Racism is real." It is impossible to see race, given that it is a vicious social construct, but it is absolutely possible (and far too frequent) to see racism. Systemic subjugation and power are not about race – they are about racism – and the historical arbitrariness (that we as a society perpetuate, "whiteness") of who is empowered, and of who is disempowered.

In the foreword Ta-Nehisi Coates (2017, xi) wrote for Toni Morrison's *The Origin of Others*, he explains this point exactly:

> "When we say 'race' as opposed to 'racism,' we reify the idea that race is somehow a feature of the natural world and racism the predictable result of it. Despite the body of scholarship that has accumulated to show that this formulation is backwards, that racism precedes race, Americans still haven't quite gotten the point."

By maintaining the language of racial difference, we perpetuate the foundation of systemic racism, and are ultimately creating a trap for ourselves in our efforts to dismantle the system.

Naturally, since the birth of my son, I have thought a great deal about this connection. In June 2015, I had the privilege to train as a National SEED Leader in San Anselmo, California, and I had the opportunity to reflect more deeply on these thoughts.

SEED (Seeking Educational Equity and Diversity) is an incredible organization that is dedicated to training educators to discuss systems of subjugation and power, and to create systemic change as a result. The training is an intense, weeklong endeavor in which participants are asked to take stock of their lived experiences and how those experiences have contributed to systemic oppression and/or to systemic dominance.

One of the mantras of SEED is to focus on "The scholarship of the shelves as well as the scholarship of the selves." This refers to the importance of teachers educating themselves intellectually as well as emotionally. Educators bring their whole selves into the classroom, so it is imperative that they understand their own truths, as well as historical and cultural truths, in order to create equitable environments.

I loved my SEED training – it was an impressive gathering of passionate and informed educators. There were many difficult moments for me that week, however, and one of the main reasons was because the language of racial difference erased my lived experience, and that of my son's.

I have always felt uncomfortable in conversations that are sweeping generalizations of individuals. Even as a child or an adolescent, I would feel protective of my father when I would hear someone state something general about "white people." I would also feel protective of my mother when I would hear someone state something general about Latin Americans or about immigrants. I was well aware of my parents' truths and their dedication to challenging racism, and I felt very protective of them in such moments.

As a mother, discussions that reify racial difference literally make my stomach turn. For example, one of the activities at my SEED training asked all of us to write a three-sentenced statement that began with, "My experience with racism is…" Once we had done so, as a whole group we were then asked to split up into three different groups – the white people, black people and mixed people/other people of color in the room. The division of the groups was broad to say the least. Within each there were a whole host of different backgrounds, languages, and worldviews. The mixed people/other people of color group was particularly broad, given that there were Latin Americans, Asian Americans, Middle-Eastern Americans, etc. in the group. I was struck by the ethnic and physical diversity within the three groups and how limiting it was to divide so many stories into three "neat" categories. As soon as we were told what groups we would be splitting up into and began rearranging the room, I felt the familiar discomfort in my stomach, wondering where in this space would my son go if he were in the room.

Nevertheless, I went to the mixed/other people of color group and each one of us, by group, was asked to read our statement aloud. I remember the black and white groups were facing each other, and the mixed/other people of color group were somewhat in the middle, facing the profiles of the other two groups. When my turn came to read, I said, "No, I'm not adopted. Yes, he is my biological son. My experience with racism is that it is the status quo." I made certain to state that racism is the status quo because from the moment it became clear that my son would be presumed to be white, I was faced with a conundrum about how to engage in dialogue about racism and identity without in essence accepting that the child I carried and brought forth was not only inherently different from me, but was also automatically entitled to a life of privilege and protection.

I encountered many moments like what I described above during my SEED training. It was common for us to be asked to split up between the black/brown people in the room and the white people in the room. Although the lived experience of a white person and a black/brown person in this society is vastly different, that reality is in part due to the ideology that we as a society perpetuate. There is no reason for white people to be automatically entitled to a life of privilege and protection other than the acceptance of an ideology of white supremacy. My son is not superior because of his physical appearance and I refuse to raise him to believe otherwise.

As I had been doing in my work at Horace Mann, at SEED training, I was unafraid to voice all of these thoughts and feelings, and as with my colleagues at Horace Mann, my SEED colleagues listened to me respectfully and kindly but could not see how we could discuss and challenge systemic racism without also discussing race.

Ta-Nehisi Coates writes in *Between the World and Me* (2015, 7) that, "Race is the child of racism, not the father." James Baldwin, in an interview once said, "It's up to you. As long as you think you're white, there's no hope for you. As long as you think you're white, I'm gonna be forced to think I'm black." (Baldwin, n.d.)

Coates's statement stands out to me because it points out so simply that race is a necessary wheel for racism to continue. Baldwin's statement highlights the destructiveness of the construct of whiteness. Whiteness, as an ideology, is absolutely essential for systemic racism to thrive. It is white people who benefit from systemic racism, so in order to truly begin undoing it we must first undo the ideology of whiteness.

A criminal justice lawyer and author named Bryan Stevenson, whose work focuses on the history of lynching and its connection to modern-day police brutality and our criminal justice system once said, "I am persuaded that we really won't eliminate the problems of discrimination in the criminal justice system, in the education system, in the employment system until we change the narrative of racial difference that we have all accepted." (Stevenson. 2016) ✹

ELEVEN

The Narrative of Racial Difference

THE "NARRATIVE OF RACIAL DIFFERENCE" that Bryan Stevenson described is what allowed for people to dismiss my brother and me as our father's biological children, and what allows for people to dismiss me as my son's biological mother. Generations after slavery, our society perpetuates the belief that skin color equates race.

I have had countless experiences of how our society's ideology of inherent racial difference has informed people's reactions to and interactions with my family. I did not recognize these moments as reflective of our country's ideology of racial difference, however, until after I became a mother.

When my son was about three years old, we were waiting on a train platform in Manhattan. I noticed a woman admiring my son. I gave her a small smile, which she returned and then, seeming to feel that I was approachable, said to me "He is so cute! How long have you looked after him?" I responded, "Since he was in utero." I did not say it snidely or dismissively – I said it with conviction, as it is the only true answer to her question. Her face became pale with embarrassment. Faltering some, she said, "Oh. He's yours? I'm so sorry."

The assumption that woman made about me being my son's caretaker, and never even entertaining the possibility that I could be his mother carries with it our history of colonialism, oppression and systemic racism.

Many people in our society are completely unaware of how the assumptions they make about others are absolutely informed by our history. Although it is exhausting to be so attuned to what the assumptions made about me and my family truly belie, I am grateful for the awareness because it does not allow a destructive ideology to define my sense of self or how I raise my son.

My father was treated for his pancreatic cancer at Columbia-Presbyterian Hospital and though he was weak, he always loved to walk so he would often go for short walks with one of us down the hospital corridors. On one of those occasions walking with my dying father, we ran into a nurse who had been caring for him but who had not yet met his family. She greeted him, never once looking at me and innocently asked, "Is this your new nurse?" My father, despite his proximity to death, mustered what little strength he had and proudly stated, "No. She's my daughter." The nurse reddened and apologized, just as the woman on the train platform had.

Both experiences, however, taught me not only of an acceptance of an ideology of racial difference but of an elevation of whiteness, and a devaluation of blackness/brownness. In both interactions, I was presumed to be an employee, and with my father, it was as if I did not exist at all.

The vastly different assumptions of my father being my adoptive father versus me being my biological son's caretaker reflect this elevation of whiteness and devaluation of blackness/

brownness. To adopt a child is an economic privilege. It also harks back to our history of colonialism, to the belief that this white man has "saved" these brown children. People would take one look at my father's skin color and one look at ours and within moments, all of these historical, cultural truths would be unmasked.

With my son, however, the assumption that I am in essence, employed by his "white" family, also speaks to the associations we have of who is privileged and empowered, as well as to our history of colonialism and oppression. My brown face tells people that I am my son's nanny as for generations black and brown women have looked after (often in fact raised) white children. Many black and brown women continue to care for (and often bring up), white children, so it is not unimaginable for people to assume I am my son's caretaker.

With that said, however, it is unacceptable. It is unacceptable that as a result of an ideology of racial difference and white supremacy, white people are more often than not in positions of power and black and brown people are not. The "narrative of racial difference" must change because it is not only the foundation of systemic racism—it is the source of its perpetuation. ❀

TWELVE

Unsolicited Questions.
Unsolicited Commentary.

THE STORIES I SHARED IN Chapter 11 are only a snippet of what I have experienced out in the world with my family. The truth is I have spent a lifetime on the receiving end of questions and comments about my existence. These come from white, black and brown people alike. The questions and comments range from sheer curiosity to outright hostility.

> "Is he a rental?" – The parent of a student when I brought Sebastián to work with me, 2012.

> "He looks nothing like you!" – Too often by too many, ongoing.

> "Tell his mother he probably won't need braces." – My son's dentist, 2017.

> "He's your son? My mother tells me I should marry a *'blanquito'* too." – An employee at Pinkberry, 2017.

> "My old nanny used to speak Spanish to me too." –A little girl at the park, after I spoke to Sebastián, 2018.

These questions and comments reveal the racial chasm in our society—the notion of an "us" and a "them."

In this society you are either white or you are not. A family like mine defies that notion. Our very existence challenges an "us and them" ideology. And rather than question the ideology, people question us. *We* are read as the problem. There can be no "us" without "them," and rather than challenge this mindset, many in our society agree to it.

I am a bilingual Ecuadorian, Jewish American. My son is a bilingual American of Ecuadorian, Jewish, Irish and German ancestry. All of my ancestors breathed life into me, and all of my son's ancestors breathed life into him. We are the essence of all of them.

> "He is not a rental. He is my son."

> "He looks quite a bit like me if you look beyond the surface."

> "I am his mother. You can tell me."

> "He is my son and he is Ecuadorian and Jewish American on my side and Irish and German American on his father's side."

> "I'm Sebastián's Mama and I've been speaking Spanish to him since he was in my belly."

The time to stop perpetuating racist narratives as if they were inherent, universal truths is long past due. ✤

THIRTEEN

Otherness

THERE IS SPECIFICITY to the curiosity and hostility my family experiences. There is also a subtlety.

In high school, I have a clear memory of a classmate asking me "what I am." I responded, "I'm half-Ecuadorian and half-Jewish." She gave me a disbelieving look and with anger, responded, "That doesn't tell me anything. What color is Jewish?" I was startled by both her words and her tone, but given my experience with such interactions and my ability to think quickly, I matter-of-factly responded, "What color is Ecuadorian?" She was silenced, as my response highlighted the ridiculousness of her question, as well as the callousness of it.

When that classmate asked me "what I am," (which in and of itself is an offensive question), she should have simply accepted my response. I know who I am, and yet, my response did not fit her notion of how one should self-define. She saw me, a brown-skinned, bilingual girl, whom she could not quite pinpoint, and so she approached me, not with openness and curiosity, but with anger and resentment.

I have written about the teasing I experienced as a child, such as being called "monkey lips." I am sadly beginning to observe a teasing of my son that I believe is rooted in our perceived otherness. Although when Sebastián is out in the world with Adam, or with his paternal family, and not with me, he is presumed to be white, the minute I show up, his complex truth is revealed. To be honest, it is revealed the minute he shares his name, but that alone is not enough to shock those around him. Even at his young age, children at the park will say, "That's your mom? You're his mom?" The narrative of skin color as definer and as equating similitude is so powerful that six-year-old and seven-year-old children have also internalized it. My son proudly states, "Yup!" And I evenly say, "I'm his Mom," and will often place my face right next to Sebastián's so that the children asking will see our facial features, our whole faces, rather than our different coloring alone.

The children will then often smile or chuckle and say, "He does look like you!" or "You have the same mouth!" Once they see past our different coloring, they see us.

Nevertheless, Sebastián is arriving at an age where these intrusive questions or the disbelief we encounter upset him. He told me recently that when people do not believe I'm his mother, it bothers him because not only am I his mother, but we do look alike. I soothed him and explained that though I know it hurts and angers him, when people ask him that, it is about them, not about us. But Sebastián is now coming home telling me of classmates who will tease him for how seamlessly he speaks Spanish. He'll tell me, "They say, 'ooh, Sebastián, you think you're so smart!'" These interactions clearly upset him, and as his mother, they hurt and upset me too. And I know in my gut that some of it, if not all of it, have their roots in his "difference."

Sebastián, like me, exists in the middle, in the nuanced world of those who belong to more than one culture and who speak more than one language. In his case, however, because he is presumed to be white, his nuance is even more confusing and unsettling to others.

The reactions we receive are not always hostile. They are sometimes sad, and revealing of how powerful our history of colonization, white supremacy and systemic racism is. I have observed that quite often, when Latin Americans meet Sebastián, they are startled that his name is in Spanish, but even more so, they are startled to discover that he speaks Spanish fluently. Their instinct is to speak to him in English, and even after it's been established that he is also a Spanish speaker, they will comment on how "good" his Spanish is, as if he were a foreigner who had studied and learned the language, as opposed to the native speaker that he is. Even if their English is not as fluent, they will address Sebastián in English. I am convinced that this has to do with his presumed whiteness. These fellow Latin Americans hear that his name is in Spanish and they hear that he is a Spanish speaker, but they cannot reconcile that with his light brown hair, blue-green eyes and light skin. They see a white *"americanito,"* (little American) and to be American, you speak English and you change your name to be more palatable to English-speaking ears. These interactions are also intricately connected to our perceived otherness and the fact that we disrupt historical and cultural narratives. They also reveal internalized racism and white supremacy.

The internalized racism and white supremacy do not only manifest in black and brown people, however. I have noticed how this internalization manifests in white people as well, and it has deeply affected my interactions with them, particularly now with Sebastián in the world.

When I was a new mother and adjusting to my role, I tried some different "Mommy & Me" type gatherings but quickly learned not only how much my son and I stood apart, but how out-of-place I felt. I was assumed to be my son's nanny, and even after it was established that I was his mother, the conversations were so often offensive to me. I would say I am half-Ecuadorian, and a fellow mother would tell me about her nanny who was from Ecuador, as if that would be a point of connection. Or once it was established that I was bilingual, I would be told something about the nanny who speaks Spanish, or was once told, "I am fluent in vacation Spanish." Perhaps these women thought they were making comments that would put me at ease, make me realize how "worldly" and "open" they were, but they served to do the exact opposite. They alienated me even further, and I have come to realize that in some ways, there are few people with whom I can feel a true connection, particularly now that I am the brown mother of a son presumed to be white.

Even now, years after Sebastián's birth, going to the park with him is emotionally and psychologically exhausting. I am one of the few brown faces who is not the nanny, in fact, and even with the other black and brown parents, I often feel a separation because Sebastián is presumed to be white. I have learned to bring a book with me to the park, especially now that Sebastián is older, and make it clear that I am not very interested in taking part in any conversation.

The parents I have connected with the most in our neighborhood parks are the parents who, like me, live between worlds and languages. These parents, though they may initially feel shocked or confused by my family, do not make me feel "othered," and with them I can find true points of connection. And these are parents who according to our American system of categorization and classification would be considered white, black or brown.

All of these experiences make me think of a passage my mother would quote to me from Zora Neale Hurston's *Their Eyes Were Watching God* (1991, 40), "Logan was accusing her of her mamma, her grand-mamma and her feelings…" When Sebastián is older I am sure I will teach him that quote, but in the meantime, it informs the lessons Adam and I are teaching him about never curtailing who he is to please other people.

My family's perceived otherness is just that – someone else's perception. We will not be accused of being who we are. ❀

FOURTEEN

Terminology

OUR SOCIETY IS OBSESSED with categories and labels, particularly when it comes to "race" and ethnicity. It is nearly impossible to fill out any form without being asked to check what "race" or ethnicity one is. For a person like me, that question can prove very unsettling. It has only grown more so since Sebastián's birth.

There is a long, ever-shifting history to the labels our Census (and other forms, but the Census in particular) has used. In 1790, on the very first United States Census there were five options:

> "Free White Males 16 years and over,"
> "Free White Males under 16 years,"
> "Free White Females,"
> "All Other Free Persons," and
> "Slaves."(Enright, 2013)

These categories remained virtually unchanged until 1820, when, for the first time, an option for "Free Colored Persons" appeared. In 1850, an option for "mulatto" appeared. "Mulatto" appeared alongside "White" and "black," under the heading of "Color." "White" was the only one capitalized. The term "mulatto" stems from "mule," which is the product of a male donkey and a female horse, animals belonging to two different species. "Mulatto" became a way to refer to the offspring of a white and black person, reifying the erroneous and hateful fiction that white and black people are inherently different.

In 1870, "Chinese" (referring to all East Asians) and "Indian" (referring to Native Americans) appeared on the Census. Note that as these categories shift, "white" remains in place, as well as separate from any other option. By 1890, options for "quadroon" (one-fourth "black ancestry"), "octoroon" (one-eighth "black ancestry") and "Japanese" appeared. "Quadroon" and "octoroon" are particularly telling as they were for individuals who had that "quantifiable" amount of black ancestry. These individuals could have had blonde hair, light skin and light eyes, but because of their known black ancestry, they were relegated to a category separate from "white." It is clear that the goal was to maintain a separate, superior status of whiteness.

Throughout the 1900s, categories continued to shift, vacillating between the use of "Color" or "Race," as well as adding in new categories, such as "Hindu, Korean and Filipino" in 1920, "Mexican" in 1930, as well as formalizing the "one drop rule," referring again to the notion that "one drop of black blood" signified that a person was black. In 1940, "Mexican" was removed and would be listed under "White." In 1960, individuals were allowed to fill out the Census form for themselves, as opposed to having a Census taker gather the information. In 1980, "Vietnamese, Asian Indian, Guamanian, Samoan, Eskimo and Aleut" were added and in 1990, "Color" was again removed, with only "Race" appearing and if one tried to check more than one, only the first one was counted. In 2000, for the first time, people were allowed to check more than one "race," which over seven million people did. In some census years, there existed an option for "some other race."

In 2010, with my infant son in my arms, I vividly remember looking at the Census options, reflecting on what categories would best describe my family. For Adam, I checked "White" and for me and Sebastián, I checked "White," "Black," "Hispanic/Latino," "Asian" and for "some other race" I wrote in "Multiethnic" for both of us.

The history of the categories used on the Census since 1790 is a glaring example of the insanity our acceptance of the narrative of racial difference has become. I have studied and examined this evolution for much of my life, but only after giving birth to a son this society presumes to be white, did I decide to reject all racialized language. I refuse to define myself or my family within racialized terms. To do so would be to accept and to reinforce the fallacy of whiteness and inherent racial difference. The only label that is truly reflective of who we are is "multiethnic." I hail from many ethnicities, many cultures, as do so many human beings, but every one of the individuals who contributed to my existence (and that of my son's) belonged to the same species. We are not "mulattos" and I refuse to give power to language that is destructive and untrue.

I remember having to fill out a form when I worked at Horace Mann that offered four options – "White," "Black," "Asian" and "Unknown." I was floored to read this and commented to the individual I was with how offensive, hurtful, reductive and inaccurate such an option was. Unknown? To whom? To myself? To others? I know exactly who I am, despite it being unclear to others. Ultimately, all "racial" categories are reductive. "White" originally from Germany, Ireland, Italy, Russia, etc., "Black" from West Africa, the Caribbean, the British Virgin Islands, etc., "Asian" from China, Japan, Korea, Thailand, etc., the list is exhaustive.

Attempting to pigeonhole human beings into separate categories meant to uphold the status quo (i.e. white supremacy) has resulted in nothing but a deeply divided, destructive and injured nation. It is this division, destruction and injury my parents were determined to avoid in raising me and my brother and what Adam and I are determined to avoid in raising Sebastián. ❀

FIFTEEN

Whiteness

WHITENESS, AS A CONCEPT and as a belief system, has been created over a long period of time, beginning in the late 1600s in order to justify slavery and the notion of an inherent racial hierarchy. (Norton, 2014) "White" people were naturally superior, and "black" people (later to include all "people of color") were naturally inferior. Despite modern science refuting race as biological, we continue to adhere to this belief system culturally.

At the White Privilege Conference in April 2016, I decided to truly challenge whiteness by attending a white affinity group meeting. I chose to attend not because I have any wish to be perceived as "white," but rather as an intentional challenge to white supremacy and systemic racism. One introductory exercise was to write our reason for being in the space and what we hoped to get out of it. I had written about my experience as a mother as succinctly as I could. When I spoke, I shared that if I were to accept an ideology of racial difference, I would create a divide between mother and son. I said perhaps it is high time dark-skinned, multiethnic people like myself lay claim to their "whiteness" as well. I said it is now clear to me that as a society, we not only perpetuate a racial divide, but we adhere to the most essential tenants of white supremacy and systemic racism.

I am often told how "lucky" I am that my son is so light-skinned. I have been told this by white, brown and black people alike. Racism (and colorism within black and brown communities) are so omnipresent that even people who are adamantly fighting against systemic racism and white supremacy will continue to perpetuate the ideologies at their base. I cringe every time I am told my son is "lucky" because "lucky" implies a number of things, all of them negative. It implies that I am then "unlucky" to have dark skin and features that hark back more clearly to Africa and to Asia. It implies that by virtue of my son's physical appearance, he is automatically entitled to a life of privilege and protection. It implies that because he is presumed to be white, he will not necessarily be harassed, or worse, killed by law enforcement officials.

I would never deny that my son's presumed whiteness does in fact protect him in this society, but it is precisely that reality that needs to change. There is no other explanation for my son's automatic protection and privilege other than an elevation of whiteness and a devaluation of blackness and brownness.

Despite knowing that my son's presumed whiteness protects him, I refuse to raise him to believe that it is acceptable. No one in this society should accept racist narratives that privilege and protect whiteness while simultaneously disenfranchising and criminalizing blackness and brownness. It is the acceptance of those narratives that gives white supremacy and systemic racism the power they require to thrive.

All of the truths about my son's privilege and protection lead directly to the seed of white supremacy and systemic racism – the creation of an ideology of racial difference and whiteness. My son should not be automatically protected by his skin color – the fact that he is, *is* the crux of our deeply racist and unjust society.

My son is no more lucky to be light-skinned than I am unlucky to be dark-skinned. To perpetuate that narrative in the raising of our children is damaging not only to their psyches but to their ability to empathize and recognize the commonality of humanity.

Resistance is what motivates me to challenge the rotten root of white supremacy and systemic racism. If I do not resist, I will relinquish agency in how I raise my son, and how I wish for him to self-conceptualize. It will also allow for my own devaluation and erasure.

The reactions that link good fortune with my son's physical appearance are reflective of internalized racism, and the notion that the lighter you are, the more worthy you are. These concepts were introduced through colonization, slavery, oppression, and dominance. And the consequences of these concepts are central to having been unfairly empowered or subjugated.

Later in the evening of the same day I joined the white affinity group meeting, people who had been in the room came up to speak with me. I remember one individual said to me, "It is uncomfortable for me to be generalized as a 'white' person. I really dislike being generalized." Another said to me that during the conference she had been "left feeling unbearably white and privileged." Some of them told me of their own dissonance associating with whiteness, given that either they themselves were immigrants or were the children or grandchildren of recent immigrants. They said how uncomfortable it is to know that by virtue of their physical appearance they are privileged and are beneficiaries of white supremacy and systemic racism. Another said to me that she had never thought about what I had brought up and it made her think of "when people are misidentified." I realized in those brief interactions that perhaps there is a whole other approach to challenging systemic racism – an approach that does not require the acceptance and perpetuation of the fallacy of racial difference.

My son is already receiving messages (which my husband and I are combating) about his supposed inherent superiority. I was once told by a shopkeeper in our neighborhood how "clean" Sebastián's skin is. He said it in Spanish, *"limpia,"* but the association is unmistakable – lightness equates cleanliness, pureness, or holiness, and darkness equates being dirty, marred, or cursed. When the shopkeeper said that to me, I responded, *"Su piel no es limpia, es clara. Eso no tiene nada que ver con la limpieza."* ("His skin is not clean, it is light. That has nothing to do with cleanliness.")

We need to stop relaying these messages of inherent difference and of attaching value to skin color, whether covertly or overtly. As I learned in my conversations the evening of attending the white affinity group meeting, the dissonance many white people feel with whiteness is ammunition for challenging the language and ideology at the base of white supremacy and systemic racism.

The scientist Bill Nye (2013) once said, "Researchers have proven scientifically, that humans are all one people. The color of our ancestors' skin and ultimately my skin or your skin is a consequence of ultra-violet light, of latitude and climate. We are one species. We have to work together!"

A statement like the one above is often scoffed at or dismissed in equity circles, or even in conversation, because it ostensibly denies the lived truth of systemic racism. I believe, however, that what Bill Nye says is crucial to both bringing the lived truth of systemic racism to light, and to challenging that very system.

The narrative and ideology of racial difference began with dehumanization and that dehumanization continues. We truly are one human family and perhaps in recognizing our shared humanity, rather than perpetuating superficial physical differences as immutable and automatic separators, we will be able to properly armor ourselves to combat white supremacy and systemic racism, and hopefully in time, to dismantle them. ✸

SIXTEEN

People Who Look Like Us

DURING MY SEED TRAINING, I learned of a concept that is essential to creating equitable classrooms. The concept – "windows and mirrors" – refers to the importance of children seeing into the worlds of others as well as seeing reflections of their own worlds. I began to notice, however, that the concept was more often than not associated with skin color.

Even before my SEED training, I would hear colleagues discuss the importance of children seeing "people who look like them" referring to skin color. Or I would hear a statement like, "Children need to see reflections of themselves. It is important for black and brown children to see black and brown families like their own." The discussion would focus on the fact that white children are accustomed to seeing reflections of themselves in the media and their schools' curricula, and African American, Latin American, Asian American, Middle Eastern American and Multiethnic children are not. This is not an untrue observation, and one I agree with, but I struggled with such statements because they emphasized the supposed "affinity" of skin color in a way that for a person like me and a family like mine does not ring true. Statements like these are also at the base of why people were incapable of seeing our father in my brother and me and why they are incapable of seeing me in my son.

Often in equity work there is a sense that if skin color is not being discussed, colorblindness is being encouraged. I disagree. Colorblindness is not the solution as it denies the lived reality of systemic racism, but color consciousness is also not the solution, as it reinforces the ideology at the foundation of the system.

Growing up, people categorically dismissed the possibility of any physical resemblance between our father and my brother and me. We would always feel insulted and taken aback, because despite our difference in coloring, there were unmistakable shared facial features. My brother in fact, with the exception of his coloring, looks so much like our father that I used to joke that he was our father dipped in milk chocolate! The reality is that we both physically resemble our father.

And over the years since Sebastián was born it's become clear that in addition to sharing my lips, he also shares my eye shape, has a similar nose, and has my exact smile. The reality is that he too physically resembles me.

As a diversity practitioner working in equity circles, I found it dangerous (as well as erroneous) to reinforce skin color not only as definer, but as a measure of similitude. It perpetuates the notion of skin color as separator. It is particularly dangerous for white children as it emphasizes their "inherent" privilege, power and protection. It also reinforces an "us and them" thinking.

My parents never engaged in talk that placed importance on the exterior and on what others would perceive. My parents always spoke to me about systems. Theirs was not a colorblind approach at all because they did discuss the difference in the value we place on light skin versus dark skin. They focused on the ideology at its root, however, rather than as an inevitable truth. My parents never discussed our varying skin tones and I am grateful every day that they did not.

Skin color should be discussed as the truth that scientist Bill Nye describes it to be—"The color of our ancestors' skin and ultimately my skin or your skin is a consequence of ultra-violet light, of latitude and climate." His statement is truly all our varying skin tones should signify.

As my parents did with me, I am intentionally avoiding teaching my son that skin color equates similitude. There have been moments when he has made a comment about a dark-skinned older woman looking like his Aba (my mother), and I am always quick to analyze with him (in age-appropriate ways) whether or not the woman he is looking at truly resembles his Aba, or if she simply shares superficial similitude, like darker skin. This awareness and intentionality is producing results because my son is able to see people's facial features and not only their skin tone.

When Sebastián was in Pre-K, for example, he drew a self-portrait of himself as brown. I did not know he had done that until a Parents' Visiting Day, and when I saw it, I was filled with pride and joy. He was four years old at the time and his drawing of himself with dark skin illustrated to me that because he is my son and a member of a multiethnic family, with varying skin tones as the norm, he sees himself as a blend of all of those people and tones, and he drew the brown shade as a result. It is kind of beautiful that my presumed to be white son, rather than being taught that his lighter coloring tells his story and is the key component of his identity, is being taught to know his totality, leading him to understand his own complexity, and to be able to understand the complexity of others as well.

I absolutely agree with the importance of "windows and mirrors" for children, but it should have to do with experiences. Children who are growing up monolingual would benefit from seeing depictions of people who speak one language as well as of people who speak more than one language. Or children who are growing up in rural areas would benefit from seeing depictions of rural as well as of city lives. Exposure to difference as well as to the familiar is crucial for children to understand themselves and others fully, but it is not and should not be about skin color. My son's drawing is proof of this.

We need to emphasize the complexity of who we are and how we came to be and through learning these truths, not only do we provide "windows and mirrors," for our children, but we encourage them to become open-minded, humble and empathic agents of change as well. ✾

SEVENTEEN

Children Must Be Carefully Taught

THERE IS A DESPERATE NEED In our society for education about the construction of racial difference, its being the root of systemic racism, as well as the construction of whiteness and its perpetuation as central to white supremacy. We are a diverse nation and it often seems to me that we have dialogues about "race" as if everyone has the same understanding of what "race" means. I am certain that they do not.

It is imperative that children "be carefully taught," in Richard Rodgers' famous words from his song, "You've Got to Be Carefully Taught" from the musical, *South Pacific,* (Rodgers and Hammerstein, 1949) that our varied physical appearances do not embody or signify meaningful differences. In teaching children about systemic racism, privilege and identity, the emphasis must always be placed on the exterior. The system is the problem – not the individual.

As my son matures, I wish for him to have a clear understanding of the crime of racism, not of the supposed crime of blackness or of darker coloring.

In my work as a diversity practitioner, I observed that although there were spaces for multiethnic children, often those spaces were still considered spaces for "children of color." It was rare to see children who could pass for white, or who were presumed to be white, in those spaces. I often wondered what messages the children were in fact receiving.

In May 2015, *New York Magazine* published "Can Racism Be Stopped in the Third Grade?" by Lisa Miller about the "racial" affinity group work happening at a New York City independent school, Fieldston. There were many passages in her article that highlighted exactly why I would push back against how this work was framed within my own school community, and within the broader scope of equity work in schools.

My brother, Nicky Enright, also feels strongly that the way the work of challenging racism in equity circles is framed upholds the basic tenants of systemic racism and is not truly setting the stage for institutional change. Although Enright is not an equity practitioner, his work as a teacher and multimedia artist has always focused on racism and identity, and he and I have often discussed what we observe. Given that we were raised in the same home by the same parents, his passion and awareness should be no surprise.

One statement in the article that both my brother and I found particularly jarring was, "We talk about how it's important to know what your race is." (Miller, 2015) To this my brother responded, "They wish to ignore the inconvenient fact that there is no such thing as race – the very fact that actually could light a path." This highlights how even the language of "racial" affinity groups is counterintuitive and counterproductive.

I believe the language of "racial" affinity groups is counterintuitive and counterproductive because it reifies the fiction of inherent difference. It reifies the lie that skin color equates "race," and it perpetuates the foundation of white suprema-

Naomi Raquel Enright

cy and systemic racism. I put "racial" in quotations precisely because it is erroneous to believe that people with a similar skin tone belong to a separate "racial" group. It is scientifically untrue, and though it has been culturally and socially true for generations, it is high time we move beyond the ethos that brought our systems of white supremacy, racism and anti-blackness into being. Reinforcing the ethos of said systems in an effort to shed light on and to change them is a vicious cycle. True systemic, cultural and social change will never come about if that cycle continues.

There was another statement in the article referring to a student saying that the groups, "...put you in a group of what race you are..." To this my brother responded, "Believing that race is real, and acting on those beliefs - that there are biological differences between people who may look different and they should be kept separate/have much in common, etc., has got to be the most basic definition of racism. 'Race-ism.'"

Enright coined his own term to describe what I had been observing as well, and which I refuse to participate in now that my son is in the world. To know that my son would be placed in the "white affinity group" based solely on his physical appearance and be told within the group that it is because of their superficial similitude that they are together is unacceptable. Not only would my son then be learning that he is inherently different from all dark-skinned people, including his own mother, but he would begin to believe that the automatic protection, privilege and power of whiteness is natural – that the world has always been and will always be this way. It has not and it should not be.

At one point the following statement appears in the article, "...this program is one step to helping a generation of kids see that racial difference is a fact of life – but doesn't have to determine a child's fate..." (Miller, 2015) To this my brother responded, "The notion of racial difference is not 'a fact of life,' it's the foundation of racism." *Exactly*.

The supposed inevitability of systemic racism and white supremacy is what needs to be reexamined and reimagined. Why should I live my life knowing that I will be unfairly devalued, dismissed and disrespected based only on my darker coloring? Why should white people live their lives knowing that they will be unfairly elevated, seen and respected based only on their lighter coloring? Why should I teach my own son that this is an acceptable reality? I shouldn't, and frankly, no child should learn that such a vastly different expectation for one's life experience, based on a superficial distinction, is acceptable.

On the whole, my brother and I were disappointed and saddened by the article. Although the program in the article had its strengths, it could have been that much more powerful if in addition to examining our vastly different lived experiences, it also examined and debunked the ideologies at the base of systemic racism and white supremacy.

I remember Enright saying to me, "The only promising thing here is encouraging young kids to feel comfortable talking about racism, but for that you absolutely do not need to segregate them according to the very categories that were created to practice racism in the first place – the very categories we need to move beyond. It's a little late to fight racism with 'race-ism'." I could not agree more with my brother. We simply cannot fight racism using the same tools that created it.

In May 2016, Enright self-published an essay entitled "Break The Cycle." In his opening he wrote:

> "In terms of racism, xenophobia, and immigration, a possible answer is that we don't get along because we are heirs to – and continue to accept – the deeply flawed ideology of race, the pseu-

do-scientific fiction that purportedly confers selective advantages and disadvantages to particular groups of human beings. Even many of us who resist racism may unwittingly continue to accept the underpinnings of its ideology and to function under its edicts. In doing so, they fight the symptoms, not the disease of racism."

"Fighting the disease, paradoxically, is both simple and complex; dismantling racism will require nothing less than a paradigm shift in our society. This may help explain why even many diversity professionals in academia, whose charge is to address institutionalized racism, tend to focus more on the symptoms, which range from micro-aggressions to profiling than on systemic racism" (Enright, 2016)

How we as a society have come to discuss and challenge systemic racism and white supremacy, then, is what ultimately has allowed for further damage. There have been many moments in our society's history to face our true founding principles, and commit not only to owning these truths, but to becoming a nation that is truly equitable.

In "Break The Cycle" my brother describes this point exactly, "The paradigm shift requires that we begin to recognize and denounce the problem at its root; that is, the myth of race-based categorization." (Enright, 2016)

My son is part of that "paradigm shift" and is being "carefully taught." Just as he drew himself with brown skin in his Pre-K self-portrait, he has no difficulty seeing our shared physical traits and in fact will often assume familial connection with people of different skin tones that he sees at the park or on screen. He has often said statements like, *"La mamá de esa niña dijo que puedo jugar con ella."* ("That girl's mother said I could play with her.") Sometimes he has been right that the adult is the child's parent, and other times he has been wrong, but he has said things like this to me frequently, regardless of the child's or adult's skin tones. He will often in fact assume that dark-skinned women or men are the parents of light-skinned children. Varying skin tones in a family is his own reality so he does not dismiss it as an impossibility.

When I have asked him what he says to people who tell him he looks nothing like me, he has said that he responds, *"Yo les digo que sí nos parecemos, que tú eres mi mamá."* ("I tell them that we do look alike, that you are my mother.") His matter-of-factness and bluntness speaks volumes. Adam and I are intentionally and carefully teaching him not to equate skin color with similitude, and as a result he is more shocked by people's inability to see our similitude rather than the fact that he is my biological son. He is not reducing people to the superficiality of their skin tones, nor is he placing value on people based on their skin color.

When Sebastián was two years old, for Christmas 2012, my brother, his Toh (his word for *"Tío"*) gave him a book entitled *Gugi, Gugi* (2004) by Chih-Yuan Chen. He gave it to him in Spanish and it has turned out to be instrumental in Adam and I carefully teaching our son. It is about a crocodile raised by ducks and how he comes to understand himself to be neither all crocodile, nor all duck, but a *"cocopato"* ("crocoduck"). The book is cute and sweet, but it is also extremely profound.

Gugi, Gugi faces adversity and pain as he realizes he is set apart from ducks as well as from crocodiles, but after some introspection, he realizes that his strength in fact lies in his truth as a *"cocopato."* He comes to peace with his multilayered identity, and realizes that ultimately it should be him who decides who he is, not anyone else.

The Sneetches (1953) by Dr. Seuss has been another book Adam and I have used to carefully teach Sebastián. *The Sneetches* was instrumental in my own childhood and has been instrumental to me as a parent as well. As a child, my parents would read *The Sneetches* to me and used it to explain prejudice, privilege and power. It is a poignant examination of the dangers of both creating an "us and them" narrative as well as of the arbitrariness of who is empowered and who is not. It is also a profound look at how such delineations affect our psyche and our subsequent behavior. ✿

EIGHTEEN

Resist Whiteness

THE WRITER GLORIA YAMATO in her essay "Something About the Subject Makes It Hard To Name" (2004, 101) describes the erasure and dilution that are the result of systemic racism, "Racism must be dealt with on two levels, personal and societal, emotional and institutional. It is possible – and most effective – to do both at the same time. We must reclaim whatever delight we have lost in our own ethnic heritage or heritages. This so-called melting pot has only succeeded in turning us into fast-food gobbling 'generics' (as in generic 'white folks' who were once Irish, Polish, Russian, English, etc. and 'black folks,' who were once Ashanti, Bambara, Baule, Yoruba, etc.)"

In that same essay she also highlights the destructiveness of believing that racism is an inescapable truth, "Racism is pervasive to the point that we take many of its manifestations for granted, believing 'that's life.'" (Yamato, 2004, 99)

After the Neo-Nazi/White Supremacist rally in Charlottesville, Virginia in August 2017, I thought a great deal about these revelations vis-à-vis the need to name and combat the ideologies of whiteness and of racial difference. Nearly all of the reports I read in response to the rally upheld both.

I read one account about a white supremacist at the rally named "Peter Cvjetanovic," who spoke of the importance of "white European culture" and "white heritage." He also claimed to not be the "angry racist" his image depicted him to be. I read his words and asked myself, when did his family become white? How many generations ago? And I wondered how he could state that there exists such a thing as "white European culture" given that whiteness is a concept born in the United States.

There is no such thing as "white heritage," or "white European culture." There is, however, such a thing as "white American culture." White American culture is absolutely a reality.

The writer Eula Biss wrote an article for *The New York Times Magazine* entitled "White Debt," which was a powerful piece highlighting the desperate need in our society to name the root of systemic racism in order to create true systemic change. At one point she writes:

> "Whiteness is not a kinship or a culture. White people are no more closely related to one another, genetically, than we are to black people. American definitions of race allow for a white woman to give birth to black children, which should serve as a reminder that white people are not family. *What binds us is that we share a system of social advantages that can be traced back to the advent of slavery in the colonies that became the United States. Whiteness is not who you are.* [Emphasis added]." (Biss, 2015)

The Unitarian Minister Rev. Dr. Carl Gregg poignantly highlights the danger of the continued construction of and belief in whiteness in his article, "What Ta-Nehisi Coates Taught Me About 'People Who Believe They Are White.'" In his introduction he states, "In the book *Learning To Be White,* the Unitarian Universalist minister and scholar Thandeka writes that, 'No one is born white in America.'" (Gregg, 2015)

In terms of the construction and perpetuation of whiteness, many white Americans, for example, have stories of ancestors who changed their surnames to be more palatable to the English-speaking tongue. My own paternal grandfather was born Abraham Epstein, and my father, Joseph Hillel Epstein. When my father was six years old and entering school, my grandfather decided that he did not want his son or his family to be identifiably Jewish, so he changed his name to Alfred Enright, and my father became Joseph Hill Enright. My mother-in-law's maiden name, Bare, was originally the German Bär. These are only two anecdotes – there are countless others just like them.

Many white Americans also know of ancestors who stopped speaking their native tongues (Italian, Hungarian, Polish, etc.) in order to assimilate to America and to ensure that future descendants would be "American." There is a process to "becoming white" and it involves steps like the ones I have just described.

Becoming a white American is to simultaneously shed one's ethnic heritage and to agree to the privilege and protection that whiteness ensures. This is not something I think individuals or families have done consciously or intentionally – it is an unspoken, unwritten understanding that whiteness is what equates power in our society. As these immigrants arrived (and continue to arrive), they learned this tacit truth, and in order to provide stability and a chance for success for their descendants, they let go of their cultural histories and grabbed ahold of whiteness. Gregg refers to this phenomenon in his article:

"Consider, for instance, how quickly the social construction of race has changed when we remember that, 'it was not uncommon in the nineteenth century for the English and Americans to regard the Irish as "black," and for Italians to have an ambiguous status between white and black in the U.S.' But today, Jewish, Italian, and Irish immigrants to this country are 'people who believed themselves to be white.' They have 'learned' – they have been pressured to socialize – into being white." (Gregg, 2015)

The reference Carl Gregg makes to how the Irish, Jews and Italians were once viewed as separate from "white" is crucial. The process to "becoming white" has varied for different European groups. And it is important to remember that it was precisely a process – it is not as if suddenly, all Europeans were considered white.

Before World War II, there were a number of European enclaves in New York City, including "Little Germany" on what is now the Upper West Side and Lower East Side of Manhattan. The individuals living in those neighborhoods then did not identify as "white," – the very notion of identifying as such would have been preposterous. They were German – speaking their language, cooking their foods, listening to their music, and feeling wholly connected to their roots.

After World War II, however, the Germans, Irish, Italians and Jews were invited into the fold of whiteness, so to speak, as a reward for fighting in the war and more importantly, as a means to maintain power.

This is much the same way more recent immigrant groups have learned to shed their languages, cultures and origins in order to be recognized as "white" and to benefit from the unearned privilege, power and protection that whiteness ensures.

It is only through looking back at history that this design is so clear. The "melting pot" we so often refer to in this country, then, is in fact an effort to maintain the status quo – that is, of white supremacy and anti-blackness. Only those who can pass for, or who are presumed to be white, can "melt" into whiteness and that is at the very specific cost of black and brown lives.

James Baldwin in his essay "On Being White...And Other Lies" described this social pressure to agree to whiteness as:

> "The crisis of leadership in the white community is remarkable – and terrifying – because there is, in fact, no white community. It bears terrifying witness to what happened to everyone who got here, and paid the price of the ticket. The price was to become 'white.' No one was white before he/she came to America. It took generations, and a vast amount of coercion, before this became a white country." (1984, 135-136)

He furthers this point with the following:

> "America became white – the people who, as they claim, "settled" the country became white – because of the necessity of denying the Black presence, and justifying the Black subjugation. No community can be based on such a principle – or, in other words, no community can be established on so genocidal a lie." (1984, 135-136)

The decision to agree to whiteness not only upholds and perpetuates white supremacy, systemic racism and anti-blackness, but it divorces individuals from their histories. The descendants of African slaves have been cut off from their roots by force, but the descendants of Europeans who grabbed ahold of whiteness have been cut off from their roots by choice. To be so disconnected from one's ancestral past is psychologically harmful. Human beings are social creatures and we yearn for community, but we cannot form or maintain community if we do not even know or recognize who we are.

At a protest rally responding to the violence and hatred in Charlottesville that took place in my neighborhood a few days later I saw a sign that read, "Resist Whiteness." I thought to myself, that is precisely what we as a society need to be doing. I am not saying people cannot or should not identify as white—my saying that would be erasure—but I am saying that people need to stop identifying with whiteness. Being white and agreeing to whiteness should not be synonymous. One is a cultural identity, the other a symbol of unearned, underserved systemic privilege, protection and power. Without whiteness, there would be no white supremacy or institutionalized oppression of black and brown people.

To identify as white, in my view, does not have to equate identifying with whiteness. White American culture is very much real and is the amalgamation of so many European cultures but that is not the equivalent of whiteness. To identify culturally as a white person should not translate to an agreement with whiteness, which is not only the root of white supremacy and systemic racism but what has allowed both to flourish for generations. To identify with whiteness is to allow the continued disenfranchisement, devaluation and criminalization of blackness and of brownness.

Imagine where our nation would be today if generations ago those same immigrant groups who had agreed to whiteness, had resisted it instead, had resisted benefiting from an inhumane system at the expense of their fellow black and brown citizens. It would be a far better nation had that happened. As far as I can tell, until we as a society name the origin of systemic racism and begin challenging said system by rejecting its ethos, we will forever be caught in a cycle where whiteness is valued and blackness and brownness are devalued.

There are concrete ways in which everyone, but especially white people, can resist whiteness. One way is to stop perpetuating the notion that whiteness and its automatic privilege and protection are inevitable.

Those individuals I spoke with after attending the white affinity group meeting were already pondering tools that would be concrete ways of resisting whiteness. In rejecting being "generalized as a white person" and disliking the feeling of being "unbearably white and privileged," they are on their way to resisting the ideology at the root of systemic racism, and through that resistance, and rejection, to challenging systemic racism at its core.

The language of racial difference implies that Sebastián is to walk through the world as a white boy, despite his whole truth, and that I am to walk through the world as a brown woman, despite my whole truth. I am supposed to want to surround myself by black and brown people who understand and support me and my experience, and my son, I suppose, would have to surround himself by white people in order to learn how to challenge systemic racism as a white person. I will have none of it.

Sebastián attends a dual language school where there is no ethnic majority. Nearly all of the administrators at his school are people of color, many of them women of color. Our son is learning that power and privilege do not only belong to white people, and that skin color does not define who we are nor, should it define what our experiences will be.

Whiteness perpetuates the empowerment of those deemed to be white and the disempowerment of those deemed to be black or brown. Whiteness erases the possibility for complexity and in many ways, erases our shared humanity. Whiteness is, as far as I am concerned, one of the greatest crimes against humanity.

My son will not "learn to be white," just as my brother and I did not "learn to be brown." No one should be taught that our varying skin tones, a superficial difference amongst human beings, signifies anything about our personhood, our worth, or expectations for our lived experience.

We need new language with phrases like: "Seeing racism," "an ideology of racial difference and the reality of systemic racism," "race is a social construct but systemic racism is real," "race has no biological basis and people who share superficial physical attributes do not belong to a separate racial group." This list is just a sample of new ideas we need to employ in order to challenge systemic racism at its root. ✤

NINETEEN

Colorless

IT IS NOT LOST ON ME THAT I am able to think the way I do and have come to hold the position that I do because my mother was raised in an educated, solidly middle-class family outside of the United States. My mother's self-concept formed in Guayaquil, Ecuador and despite her now having spent the bulk of her life in the United States, those formative lessons about who she is have remain unchanged.

In my equity work, it struck me more than once how often my colleagues insisted that "colorblindness" and statements like, "I don't see color" reinforce white supremacy and systemic racism. When I would discuss my concerns about the language and ideology of racial difference and whiteness with my colleagues, this was generally the response I was met with. I would often comment that although I agree that colorblindness is not a solution to the racist ills of our society, neither is color consciousness. The fact that the work to challenge and dismantle white supremacy and systemic racism reinforces the same elements that brought those systems forth is mind-boggling to me. Our skin color is not and should not be viewed as automatic definer, affinity and separator. Color consciousness is exactly what allows people to dismiss my family so quickly and easily. As a result of this society's obsession with skin color, a family like mine is viewed as otherworldly, as if we really are from a different planet.

Throughout my life, but particularly since giving birth to Sebastián, I have spoken with my mother about this obsession with skin color. My mother, when I was growing up, used to joke that she saw herself as white people are taught to in this society—as whole, worthy and capable simply by virtue of being who they are. She used to tell me that when she was growing up, she would never see the varying skin tones in her family or in her society as signifying anything, let alone defining the existence of and expectations for people's lives.

In recent years, when we speak of these issues, my mother has told me that ultimately she sees herself as "colorless," and she is very emphatic that I not focus on skin color in discussions about identity with Sebastián. She is adamant that because she and my father did not focus on skin color, my brother and I were able to self-conceptualize differently. It is that approach that has allowed us both to arrive at a place where we realize that focusing on skin color and using language that reifies whiteness and racial difference are in truth an acceptance of and an adherence to white supremacy and systemic racism.

I have no doubt that there are many who would scoff at my mother's decision to view herself as "colorless"—they probably would think it means my mother is unaware of the hatefulness and destructiveness of white supremacy, systemic racism and anti-blackness. But on the contrary, my mother's vision of herself as "colorless" is an absolute rejection of the status quo, which is to uphold the ethos at the foundation of

Naomi Raquel Enright

white supremacy and systemic racism. For my mother to define herself as "colorless" is powerful and her (and my father) having raised me to reject skin color as definer, affinity and separator is without a doubt what enables me to stand firmly by my convictions.

In our society there is a belief not only that there is an inherent difference between white people and everyone else, but that whiteness truly does translate to automatic protection, privilege and power. The reactions to my son's physical appearance solidify this mindset. The fact that people believe he is ostensibly "lucky" and immediately protected from police violence, suspicion and doubt *based solely on his coloring* absolutely corroborates the acceptance in this society of the ideologies at the bedrock of white supremacy and systemic racism.

Recently, I was telling someone how uncomfortable I often feel when my family is in Ohio visiting my in-laws. The stares, shock, and disbelief we encounter in New York is about tripled, if not more, when we are in Cincinnati. My response to this is to often stay home reading. I have more than once sent my family on an outing without me precisely because I am in no mood to be gawked at. I remember once telling Adam when he asked if I wanted to go to the zoo, "Thanks but no thanks. If I go, we'll become the exhibit." I was not exaggerating. As I shared all of this, the person I was speaking with responded, "But you're not that black."

The response startled me and I did not quite know what to make of it. I sat with it for several days and eventually came to the realization that the statement is another example of the acceptance in our society of the supposed inherent superiority of whiteness. The statement reveals the belief, albeit subconscious, that the closer one is to whiteness, the less one will suffer discrimination. The person I was speaking with was genuinely surprised that I, with my lighter brown coloring, and with my white husband and presumed to be white son (and white in-laws) would feel so keenly the sting of racism. I also think perhaps the person, again subconsciously, has come to expect the sting of anti-blackness and white supremacy as inevitable. It is the supposed inevitability of anti-blackness, white supremacy and systemic racism that we must collectively challenge as we aim to change the inequities in our society. True change will *never* come in this society if our ethos endorses the ideology of whiteness and the narrative of racial difference.

When I spoke about this conversation with Adam, I told him that so many of the reactions I receive to Sebastián's physical appearance translate to a belief that by virtue of my son's presumed whiteness, he has access to the keys to the castle, so to speak.

I have an image in my mind of an adult Sebastián entering said castle and being told, "Right this way, Mr. Whittaker." No ID, no credentials, nothing else necessary. Just his presumed whiteness. My image is an exaggeration, to be sure, but it is not entirely off the mark. The attachment of automatic protection, privilege and power with whiteness (or presumed whiteness) are the keys to the castle. And those keys should not be given out based on a destructive, dehumanizing lie. ✵

TWENTY

We Are Here

I QUOTED POET, ESSAYIST AND FEMINIST Adrienne Rich at the beginning of this book because her words echo my life experience. As she poignantly stated, "When someone with the authority of a teacher, say, describes the world and you are not in it, there is a moment of psychic disequilibrium, as if you looked into a mirror and saw nothing. Yet you know you exist and others like you, that this is a game done with mirrors. It takes some strength of soul – and not just individual strength, but collective understanding – to resist this void . . . and to stand up, demanding to be seen and heard." (Rich, 1986)

Motherhood is a redefinition of the self. In the wee hours of the morning the day after my son was born, I awoke with a start, feeling terror at the realization that I was now responsible for this human being's very survival. Nevertheless, I dove into my role as his mother, and with each passing day, fell more in love with this person Adam and I had conjured from ourselves. I also relished in watching our parents dote on their first grandchild.

When my father's diagnosis made it clear that his death was imminent, I began to feel the ever-present disequilibrium of not seeing families like mine reflected in the world, but also of knowing that I would be raising my son without the physical presence of my father.

Yet, as Rich states, I knew that I (we) existed and that it would take "some strength of soul to stand up, demanding to be seen and heard." (Rich, 1986, 199) In the years since my father's death and my son's birth, I have proven to myself that I do possess that "strength of soul." I always have, but nothing in life had tested me like the confluence of becoming a mother and a fatherless daughter.

Since both transformative experiences, I have had many moments of weakness, of doubt and of sadness. I have often wondered if I will in fact be able to resist the ideology of racial difference and whiteness in raising Sebastián, and naturally, countless times since my father died, I have wished to consult with him about all of this. I have yearned for his advice and wisdom, as well as yearned for the context he provided for my son and me.

Those moments of sadness have absolutely led to "psychic disequilibrium." Despite those moments, however, I am determined not to let the darkness overcome me. I cannot allow it to. Not only did my own parents have to resist negativity in the raising of their children but the "strength of soul" I possess I owe entirely to them. It requires tremendous psychic energy, stamina and determination to raise children like my brother and me to believe ourselves to be whole in a society that in many ways simply cannot conceive of people like us, or a family like ours, existing.

In this society, there is a "racial" binary, a black/white paradigm and the ever-present "us and them" mentality. I have been told throughout my life, that you are either one or the other.

Many multiethnic people experience this rejection – being told relentlessly that they cannot identify with the totality of their being because our society is not set up to allow them to. It is true that our society is not set up to allow me to identify as the multiethnic, bilingual individual that I am, and that it is certainly not set up to allow my presumed to be white son to identify as multiethnic and bilingual, but that does not mean that I do not, or that Sebastián will not. I will not reject all that I am through the white, Jewish father who gave me life and I will not raise Sebastián to reject all that he is through me. My brown skin did not separate me from my father and it does not separate me from my son. There may very well exist a "racial" binary, a black/white paradigm, an "us and them" mentality in this society but I refuse to curtail my own existence or experience at the behest of a system built to separate and subjugate.

My drive to share my family's truth is born out of the "strength of soul" my parents instilled in me and wishing for my son to understand that the "psychic disequilibrium" he will often experience is not about who he is, but rather about history, culture and context.

There are times since Sebastián's birth that I have felt guilt about raising him to stand apart even more than he already does. But in the long run, despite the difficulty he will experience, he will be better off. He will understand all that conspired to create him, and I hope he will honor every aspect of that history.

I have had to find concrete ways to heal from my traumatic loss and its connection to motherhood and my daily experience with racism, and writing this book is one of them. This book honors my deceased father and all he gave to me, as well as gives my son the gift of knowing his Abo, of knowing his full truth. James Baldwin once said, "If you know from whence you came, then there is really no limit to where you can go."(Baldwin, 1963, 8)

Sebastián and I may have been robbed of my father, but without him, neither of us would exist, and as my father taught me, I must let my light shine. One of my father's favorite songs was "This Little Light Of Mine," a song that since his death has taken on even more significance. Telling my family's story, sharing our truth, is letting our light shine. It is keeping the embers of my father's light aflame. We are here. ✳

TWENTY-ONE

Roots and Wings

I HAVE ALWAYS BEEN INTERESTED in knowing people's stories—who they are and how they came to be who they are. I have of course always been interested in my own history, but truth be told, I am interested in our collective history as well.

My parents and brother gave me for my twentieth birthday a canvass with a painting made by my brother that included the Baldwin quote in Chapter 20, as well as my paternal grandfather's papers from when he arrived at Ellis Island from Antopol, Russia in 1910 and my maternal great-grandmother's Last Will and Testament. The gift illustrated my deep love for family and history and the awareness that so much of who we are and how we see ourselves and the world around us is informed by both.

Another quote my father would often refer to in my childhood and adolescence was from the Spanish philosopher, George Santayana who once said, "Those who cannot remember the past are condemned to repeat it." I grew up understanding that we as individuals and we as societies are not blank canvasses – that we carry within us the failures and successes of previous generations and that we have the choice of what truths to pass down as well. My understanding of the collectiveness of humanity has been instrumental in my ability to both understand myself as well as others. It has also been instrumental in my ability to empathize.

Growing up it was typical of me to ask about our family's history as well as the cultural and societal histories of the United States and Ecuador. From a young age, in fact, I was known to be the family historian. I knew full names, birthdays, and details about the many branches of our family tree. When I was about eight years old, a family friend bought me a book about genealogy, knowing how fascinated I was to learn more about where I came from.

As a child I struggled with math, insisting throughout first grade that two plus two equaled five (the stubbornness!), but when it came to understanding genetics, my math was on point. I struggled with multiplication and division in school but as soon as I sat down to map out my family tree, I could figure out without any assistance that I shared one-quarter, or 25 percent of the same ancestry as my second cousins, for example. It always bewildered my parents, but it was clear that the math was secondary to the interest in genealogy and genetics. A good friend of mine once joked that "Naomi" in Swahili means, "Good with numbers," knowing that the only context in which I felt comfortable with mathematics was within the context of dates, genealogy and genetics.

I have carried these passions into adulthood and for Christmas 2009, our first Christmas together as husband and wife, Adam gave me a gift that would be the catalyst for my desire to nurture this passion even further. That year he presented me with a kit from the National Genographic Project, to test my Mitochondrial DNA. We all carry our matrilineal Mitochondrial DNA, but only women can pass it on to their offspring. It is one of the surest ways then to trace the origins, the dawning, of one's maternal line. I sent mine in thinking it might reveal that my maternal line is Native American, but I was fairly convinced that it would trace back to Africa. When I received my results and learned that my Mitochondrial DNA in fact originates in East Asia, I was amazed. That fell in line with my thought that it might be Native American (the Bering Strait and all Native Americans originating in East Asia), but it was still incredible to know where my maternal line began. Doing that DNA test opened Pandora's box for me in terms of wishing to know even more about my genetic origins.

For my thirty-eighth birthday, in February 2016, Adam gave me the full DNA test from 23AndMe.Com. Swabbing my cheek for this test would reveal my paternal and maternal genetic origins. I sent the test kit away, full of anticipation and excitement, and awaited my results. I knew it would take many weeks, though, so as the weeks passed, I did not forget about it, but it was not at the forefront of my mind.

On May 9, 2016, I was preparing to do a Cultural Share with an eighth grade class I was co-teaching on identity at Horace Mann. I had brought in pictures of my family (parents, brother, husband and son) and was prepared to share the family mottos I grew up hearing and extrapolated all of that to the complexity of identity. I remember sitting outside of the classroom preparing to give my presentation when I decided to check my email and lo and behold, in my in-box were my 23AndMe genetic reports. I was thrilled that on the very day I had planned to do my Cultural Share, these long-awaited results arrived.

I eagerly opened the results and was stunned by what I found. It turned out that genetically, I am 63 percent European, 19.5 percent Sub-Saharan African and 14.4 percent East Asian and Native American. Within my European results, I am 49.2 percent Ashkenazi Jewish and 10.8 percent Southern European. Within my African results, I am 18.1 percent West African and within my East Asian/Native American results, I am 11.7 percent Native American.

As I read my genetic reports, it dawned on me just how much of my son's "whiteness" is also genetically inherited from me. Genetically I am more European than anything, despite my darker phenotype. As I read the results, I quite literally felt the presence of all of my ancestors. It gave me chills and even as I write about the memory, I feel those same chills again. Baldwin's quote in that moment took on an even greater significance in my life.

Although some people argue that genetic testing is problematic vis-à-vis discussing and understanding racism and identity, I personally believe it is a sure way of combating the ancient, erroneous notion that there is inherent biological difference between human beings of different hues. I am no more closely related to other "brown" people than I am to "white" people. My skin color tells people in this society that I am brown, but my genetic results tell a vastly different (and more holistic) story about where I originate from and who I am. If used correctly, I think genetic testing can be an incredible tool to combat systemic racism and white supremacy.

Needless to say my Cultural Share was enhanced by my genetic reports, and I felt empowered on that day in a way I never had before, particularly since becoming a mother. On that day I had tangible information to explain my son's physical appearance. I had always known he had inherited European ancestry from me too, but until receiving my genetic report, I had not known how much. Adam is nearly, if not absolutely 100 percent European and I am more than 50 percent European. Naturally the child we would create together would physically resemble the bulk of his genetic inheritance. Learning of my genetic origins armored me even further.

Despite my darker coloring and my son's lighter coloring, we are both bilingual, multiethnic, international people and just as I was raised to know this (regardless of how other people perceived me), so too are Adam and I raising Sebastián to know all of who he is. People tend to dilute Sebastián as "white," and for me to be perceived and defined as "brown" is also a dilution. It is that dilution and ultimately that dehumanization that my family combats.

This perspective of mine is further solidified by Dr. Henry Louis Gates Jr.'s PBS program, *Finding Your Roots*. On that program, Dr. Gates interviews a wide range of celebrities about their family histories and will often test their DNA as well. More than once on his show guests have been amazed to discover their genetic origins—learning that they were either more or less European, African or Asian/Native American than they had been led to believe. More than one guest has in fact made a comment about how "crazy race is" when you take into account the complexity we all carry within our cells.

I watch *Finding Your Roots* religiously because it provides necessary "windows and mirrors" for me, and I believe it ought to be required viewing. I learn a great deal from every episode, about history throughout the world, but when I watch it, I also see my family's complexity and truth legitimized. People like us and families like ours are not so uncommon after all, and the more we as a culture, as a society, name this and commit to understanding it, the better off our human family (and our future) will be.

When I used the program in my "Beyond Race" elective at Manhattan Country School, just as it has done with me, it opened my students' eyes to the dehumanization that has been the ideology of racial difference and whiteness. My students began to think more broadly about who people are – their personal and familial histories as opposed to their superficial appearance. To define another person based on their hue is, as my brother reflected upon in his essay, the very basis of racism. We do not know anything about a person based on their skin color and we must collectively decide to end the generations-old habit of reducing people to their skin colors, as well as to either elevating or devaluing them based on their skin color. My students were able to understand this after watching and discussing *Finding Your Roots*. As one of my students wisely stated, we continue to believe in the idea of race. And what is worse, we act upon that belief, perpetuating the system as it was intended to be.

> "First they came for the Socialists, and I did not speak out—
> Because I was not a Socialist.
>
> Then they came for the Trade Unionists, and I did not speak out—
> Because I was not a Trade Unionist.
>
> Then they came for the Jews, and I did not speak out—
> Because I was not a Jew.
>
> Then they came for me—
> and there was no one left to speak for me."[1]

There is no "us and them." There is only "us." ❀

---

1.   Niemöller, Friedrich Gustav Emil Martin (1892-1984). This quotation is attributed to Niemöller, a Lutheran Minister and early Nazi supporter who was later imprisoned for opposing Hitler's regime. The quotation stems from Niemöller's lectures during the early postwar period. Different versions of the quotation exist. This version is engraved in a marble stone plaque at the New England Holocaust Memorial in Boston, Massachusetts.

TWENTY-TWO

Revolutionaries

MY MOTHER AND FATHER took their role as parents very seriously. My dad used to tell me that parenting is "the toughest job you'll ever love." He also once wrote that parenting is "the perfect mixture of drudgery and magic." My parents raised us to know that we were loved, that our voices mattered, and that no one else could tell us who we were.

Now that I am a mother, I know exactly why it is "the toughest job I'll ever love" as well as how accurate the description of it as "drudgery and magic" is. Parenting is hard—constant and exhausting. But it is important work because as much as we love our children, we are raising them to know who they are and to one day live in a world without us.

When my father arrived in Ecuador in 1965, he immersed himself in the culture and language. He told me that he fell for my mother because unlike many of his students, her classmates, she did not fawn over him being a white American. She told me it embarrassed her to see how her classmates behaved and that she was there to study English, nothing more. It was her aloofness that caught my father's attention.

Soon after becoming a couple, my mother won a scholarship to study at Tulane University in New Orleans. For a year she would be in Louisiana and my father in Guayaquil. Not until my adulthood did I realize what bravery and strength it took for my mother to leave Ecuador, and come to study at age nineteen in 1965 Louisiana. My mother told me that she understood the history behind the racism she experienced in this country because in her home discussions about racism and identity were also commonplace. Her parents armored her, perhaps somewhat unknowingly, but they did.

My Abuelita, for example, never bought white dolls for my mother or my aunt precisely because she did not want them to internalize a sense that there was something wrong with their own darker coloring. This was 1950s Ecuador. When I heard that story, I was amazed. My mother tells me she thinks my Abuelita made that decision after reading about Dr. Kenneth B. and Mamie Phipps Clark's 1940s doll study. It is incredible to think that my Ecuadorian grandmother was reading about an American study focusing on the devastating effects of white supremacy, systemic racism and colorism. Her awareness enhanced my mother's strong sense of self.

My mother remembers that at Christmas, her single-sex school would always have a performance and choose a little girl to be the *"Princesita de Navidad"* ("Christmas Princess"). My mother said it never escaped her attention that the girl chosen every year was also the lightest-skinned. She knew she would never be chosen to be the *"Princesita de Navidad,"* but she also knew that it was not because of her darker coloring that she would not be chosen, but rather because of institutionalized and internalized racism. She would have never had that clarity without her parents' informed and proactive approach. It is clear that I come from a long line of individuals unafraid to question and challenge the status quo.

When I received my dark-skinned cabbage patch doll, Betsy Alexandra, for Christmas 1983, I exclaimed with excitement that she reminded me of my mother and less than two months later, in February 1984, for my sixth birthday, my parents bought me a white, male cabbage patch doll. These two dolls came to represent my parents and having them was the equivalent of looking into a mirror and seeing my own home reflected. I named the boy Jeffrey Joseph and both cabbage patch dolls came to college with me and remain in my possession. They are now in my son's room and reflect the same mirror for him that they did for me.

My parents, from the onset of their relationship to their final year together, experienced racism. My own paternal grandparents disapproved of their union, focusing on the typical (yet misguided) "concern" about the children. My parents were not only deeply in love; they were also determined to write their own story.

In my family, I have always been the quickest to express anger when faced with disbelief or hostility. I have clear memories of saying out loud, after catching people staring at my father and us, "Wow! Isn't it crazy that parents and children can have different skin colors? Insane! How did that happen?" My parents and brother were often embarrassed by how quick I would voice my displeasure, but they also accepted that this was simply part of my personality, and part of how I dealt with the unnecessary attention.

Sebastián is very similar to me in this way. Once he became verbal but before he could speak in fully formed sentences, whenever he would catch people staring at us, he would look directly at the person, point to me, and say, "Mama." I could not have been more proud in those moments.

My paternal grandparents lived in Boca Ratón, Florida when I was growing up, and more than once rather than fly down to see them, we would drive, which meant driving through the South in order to arrive. My mother would always feel nervous on these trips, knowing how much more blatant the racism could be in the South than in New York City.

One year, on our way back to New York from Florida, our car broke down in the small town of Darien, Georgia. We were stranded in Darien for a week, staying at a small, local hotel. My mother, feeling unsafe in the town, refused to leave our hotel room other than going across the street to the library or to eat at the diner next door to our hotel. During that week, I would go to the library and diner as well, but I would also go for short walks (less than a mile) with my father. I remember feeling anxious and angry as we were stared at with expressions of curiosity, disapproval and outright hostility. My father would tell me to ignore these stares, and continue whatever conversation we were engaged in.

At the library and diner, as we became regulars over the course of the week, we would chat with the librarians and waitresses and owner of the diner. We shared tidbits of our lives with each other and slowly over the course of that week we became real to each other. Even the stares dissipated on our walks. They did not disappear, but I found myself feeling less anxious and less angry.

While there, as a family, we would discuss how people were interacting with us, as well as discuss our anxiety about being stranded in such a small, Southern, white town as a multiethnic and bilingual family. I was eleven years old at the time, in fifth grade, and had been engaging in such reflections my entire life so I felt prepared to deal with the situation we found ourselves in. During that time, I learned the benefit of my parents and brother's more generous natures. They were

Naomi Raquel Enright

much more friendly with the people we were meeting, whereas I was much more suspicious and retreating. When my mother would leave the hotel room, she too would extend kindness to those she came across. I began to notice how people responded, for the most part, in a similar fashion and slowly relaxed.

That week was pivotal for me in understanding that so much of racism has to do not only with ignorance, but also with a lack of exposure. This is particularly the case in overwhelmingly homogenous communities. If you never come into contact with people who identify differently than you, it is so much easier to believe narratives created to divide and conquer.

James Baldwin suggests that racism reflects a failure of empathy. In Nathaniel Rich's article, "James Baldwin & the Fear of a Nation," he states, "He [Baldwin] rejected political labels, sexual labels, and questioned the notion of a racial identity, an 'invention' of paranoid, infantile minds. 'Color is not a human or a personal reality,' he wrote in *The Fire Next Time*. 'It is a political reality.'" (Rich, 2016)

I will never forget the day we were able to leave, as we said our goodbyes, one of the librarians, in her very Southern drawl enthusiastically said, "Y'all bettah come back now, ya heah?! 'Cause we like family now!"

That librarian was right. We are family—the human family—and it was through breaking down barriers that the individuals we met were able to see our shared humanity. Our family, our story, became real to them, just as they became real to us, and all of us were forever changed as a result.

Part of what brought my parents together was their dedication to social justice. This dedication only magnified with the arrival of my brother and me. My parents were in fact sprayed with tear gas for protesting the Vietnam War in April 1971, when my mother was pregnant with my brother. Growing up my brother and I attended more than one protest with our parents, solidifying for us our determination to create change where and when we could.

I have two very vivid memories of my fearlessness to speak up as a young child. Both involve my writing letters of protest. As a child, I loved the books *The Babysitters Club* series as well as *The Sweet Valley High* series. Over time, however, I realized that *The Sweet Valley High* series did not have one single multi-ethnic character, and to add insult to injury always emphasized the lightness of the main characters' skin, hair and eyes. Nearly every book began with a description of their porcelain skin, long, blond straight hair, and bright blue eyes. Since it was a series, some repetition is to be expected, but even so I began to feel very discomfited by its focus on whiteness, as well as the fact that there were never any black or brown characters. It particularly stood out in contrast to *The Babysitters Club,* which had more than one character of color, as well as examined other issues of difference, such as divorce or the loss of a parent. I complained of this stark contrast to my parents, who naturally encouraged me to write a letter to the author. I did as they advised, and sent off my letter protesting the lack of ethnic diversity, and the emphasis on whiteness as the standard for beauty.

For many weeks, I did not receive a response, and when I did, it was a standard response to a fan letter so the author had either not read my letter or chose to disregard it. Despite the lack of follow-up from the author, I felt empowered writing that letter, and from that point on, never again purchased or read a book in the series. The author could not conceive people of color as living, breathing, and believable characters, which meant she could not see me, and I already knew I would not be rendered invisible.

The same is true for the second letter I wrote, at the age of thirteen. That was the last year I asked for a doll, a newborn, dark-skinned baby doll. I remember anxiously awaiting its arrival. When it did arrive, however, I was deeply upset and disappointed to discover that the doll resembled a baby chimpanzee. I immediately felt it was racist and told my parents so. They looked at the doll and agreed with me, so I sat down to write the doll company a letter. In my letter I told them that there was no reason for this dark-skinned baby doll to resemble a chimpanzee more than a human being and that as a dark-skinned person, I took personal offense to the doll's appearance.

This time, after a few weeks, I did receive a direct response, apologizing for how the doll's appearance had made me feel and promising that there was never any intent to associate the appearance of the dark-skinned doll with that of a primate. It was a thoughtful response, and another moment where I felt proud of my refusal to be silenced in the face of indignation.

Growing up, I also regularly heard three phrases that I believe were another key factor to me being able to see further, as well as to my strong sense of self. One of them my father would repeat like a mantra, in English, and the other two my mother would do the same, but in Spanish.

My father would always say to me, "Keep an open mind." His insistence upon the importance of recognizing that we may be wrong about a person or a situation, as well as openness itself as integral to compassion and understanding, were instrumental to my sense of self and to the world around me.

At the Remembrance Ceremony after his death, I wrote and read a tribute that began with those very same words. I spoke of how my father's openness is what led to my very existence, and that of my son's, and how he taught me to look at the world with new eyes each day. I read that I plan to teach Sebastián to do the same, to look at the world with wonder. It was a profound mantra to hear nearly every day of my childhood.

My mother would always say, *"A mi nadie me ningunea,"* which loosely translates to, "Nobody demeans me." and *"Pisa fuerte y habla recio,"* which loosely translates to "Step boldly and speak up." Her own father, my Abuelito, who died before I was born, would always quote these phrases to her and they too were powerful mantras to hear nearly every day of my childhood.

Joseph Hill Enright and Pilar Alejandrina Alava Mestanza, as it turns out, did write their own story and now I am writing mine. I am continuing the revolution. ✸

Be The Change

I T IS WIDELY BELIEVED that Mahatma Gandhi once said, "Be the change you want to see in the world." As he wisely advised, I am being the change I want to see.

I also want to share my approach to be the change with families and educators. Often existing on the fringe is necessary to being able to see a situation clearly. The fact that I live between cultures and between languages has ultimately been an advantage when it comes to understanding systemic racism and its perpetuation.

Bonnie Tsui illustrates in her article "Choose Your Own Identity" what I have described above: "In the experience of being an 'other,' there's a valuable lesson in consciousness: You learn to listen harder, because you've heard what others have to say about you before you even have a chance to speak." (Tsui, 2015)

As a result of existing as an "other," I can give families and educators new tools for rejecting the language and ideology of racial difference and of whiteness, and help them to understand that said rejection is central to the work of challenging systemic racism and white supremacy.

One main way families and educators can reject the language and ideology of racial difference and whiteness is to understand said language and ideology and to openly discuss them with their children and students.

Carl Gregg notes in his article about Ta-Nehisi Coates's *Between The World And Me*, "The problem is not children's natural curiosity about genuine differences of appearance. Instead, the problem – a problem rotting at the core of our society – is the choice to continue passing down, generation after generation, cruel lies about skin color representing anything more than superficial differences between human beings, who are in truth all members of the same extended family." (Gregg, 2015)

With my previous paragraph in mind, below is a typical discussion I would hear in my equity work: "People of all races need to come together to fight systemic racism. White people in particular have to step up to create change because black and brown people need their allyship."

With an intentionality to reject the language and ideology of racial difference and whiteness that statement would instead be as follows: "Every human being needs to come together to fight systemic racism. Those who have benefited from whiteness in particular have to step up to create change because those who have been oppressed as a result of whiteness need their allyship."

Intentionality is crucial because without it, we default to the language we have always known, which perpetuates the fallacy of racial difference and whiteness. Without an absolute paradigm shift, we as a society are simply adhering to, as well as accepting, the ideologies that created our destructive system of racism and white supremacy.

Naomi Raquel Enright

One of the responsibilities of a SEED facilitator is to host monthly seminars in their school communities that examine systems of oppression and dominance and engage in exercises that allow participants to understand said systems, and to learn tangible strategies for challenging said systems.

The exercises in a SEED Seminar are emotionally intense, and both physical as well as intellectual. There are exercises like journaling, pair sharing, chalk talks (writing ideas and thoughts collectively on a piece of chart paper), reading personal testimonies, watching *Ted Talks* and other videos about identity, and always ending a seminar with a "Circle of Appreciation."

I think in a seminar focused on challenging systemic racism and white supremacy, it would benefit participants to dissect readings about racial difference and whiteness, as well as to ask participants who identify as white to reflect on their families' stories of when during our country's history they became white. This activity would allow participants who have benefited from whiteness to reflect on why whiteness was necessary for systemic racism to come into existence, and why it has been necessary for systemic racism to thrive.

Participants who identify as African American, Latin American, Asian American, Middle Eastern American, or as multiethnic would be asked to reflect on how the construction of whiteness affects their lived, daily experience in this country. This activity would allow participants who suffer daily because of white supremacy to reflect on how whiteness is a myth and how its continued construction is necessary for black and brown people to remain disenfranchised and disempowered.

From these two activities what is known in SEED as a "fishbowl" activity would ensue in which all participants are seated in one large circle and within that circle two to three chairs are placed where individuals engage with each other about the topic at hand and the outside circle simply listens and observes.

Participants enter and leave the inner circle as they feel inspired or moved to do so. These fishbowl activities are transformative and, in my mind, fishbowling a discussion about the ideology of racial difference and whiteness would be part of a paradigm shift. Most people in our society simply do not engage in this kind of reflection and such a reflection is essential to the work of undoing systemic racism.

Peggy McIntosh, who founded the SEED Project, and who wrote the seminal 1989 article "White Privilege: Unpacking the Invisible Knapsack" (and whom I admire and respect deeply) said during my SEED training, "SEED is a spiritual process, and a reconstruction of the soul." She could not be more right and what could be more reconstructive to the soul than the rejection of the ideology created to divide and conquer, and to dehumanize?

In her article, "White Debt," Eula Biss comments on Claudia Rankine's article, "The Condition of Black Life is One of Mourning," for *The New York Times Magazine* after the June 2015 Charleston church massacre.

> "Sitting with her essay in front of me, I asked myself what the condition of white life might be. Hearing the term 'white supremacist' in the wake of that shooting had given me another occasion *to wonder whether white supremacists are any more dangerous than regular white people, who tend to enjoy supremacy without believing in it.* [Emphasis added] " (Biss, 2015)

Biss's statement is particularly poignant. The "supremacy" all "regular white people" enjoy is exactly why we cannot continue to perpetuate the ideology of whiteness and racial difference. That "supremacy" is what Sebastián is expected to benefit from and "enjoy" solely because of his presumed whiteness. There was a time in our history when whiteness literally equated full humanity, and though that is no longer true, the belief in the superiority, the protection and the privilege of whiteness continues.

"Regular white people" need to stop receiving the message that they are "inherently superior." White privilege is undoubtedly real, and part of that privilege is perpetuated because we insist on accepting an ideology of whiteness.

I remember during my SEED training, all of us were asked to answer the following questions, "What's keeping you from believing that the problem is us? What's keeping folks of color from working together? What do I need from other people of color that will enable me to trust them?"

My answer to the first question was, "Nothing is keeping me from believing it. I know it in my soul that the problem is an unwillingness to own our history, an acceptance of the framework set in place during slavery, and a resistance to acknowledge that this work takes all of us."

My answer to the second question was, "I think this is intimately tied to colonization, oppression and white supremacy. Because of them people of color are in fact in competition with one another. I also think this is because the concept of being a person of color is uniquely American and so many immigrants to this country have a different self-concept. They view themselves in national terms rather than as a color."

My answer to the last question was, "I need them to not dismiss the totality of my being and not dismiss my identification as Jewish American as well as Ecuadorian. I need them to not judge my differing perspective because of the father I had as well as the son I have."

White people should wish to relinquish whiteness because for generations, it has diluted their own ethnic truths and has allowed them to benefit from a system literally built upon the backs of black Americans, and other people of color:

> "*Race Traitor* articulated for me the possibility that a person who looks white can refuse to act white, meaning refuse to collude with the injustices of the law-enforcement system and the educational system, among other things. This is what Noel [Ignatiev, *How The Irish Became White*] called 'new abolitionism.' John Brown was his model, and the institution he was intent on abolishing was whiteness." (Biss, 2015)

This is what it would mean to relinquish whiteness. And this is how Adam and I are raising Sebastián. He most certainly looks white, but he is not being raised to collude with the injustices of systemic racism and white supremacy.

Whiteness is the ultimate form of dehumanization and erasure of one's own totality as well as of others' totality. And I have no doubt that whiteness is not an identity, but rather a corruption and an erosion of one's moral compass. Biss states:

> "'Her choice to give up whiteness was a privilege,' Michael Jeffries wrote of [Rachel] Dolezal in *The Boston Globe*. Noel [Ignatiev] said to me, 'If giving up whiteness is a privilege, what do you call hanging on to it?' As Dolezal surrendered her position in the N.A.A.C.P. and lost her teaching job, I thought of the white police officers who killed unarmed black people and kept their jobs. *That the penalty for disowning whiteness appears more severe than the penalty for killing a black person says something about what our culture holds dear.*" [Emphasis added] (Biss, 2015)

Indeed. Our culture without a doubt holds whiteness dear, as is evidenced by the expectations for my son's lived experience.

The default of his presumed automatic power, privilege and protection are born out of a belief in the sanctity of whiteness.

I believe there are many tangible ways in which we as a society can begin to challenge racism at its root and be part of the desperately needed paradigm shift to truly begin the undoing of systemic racism. To build a post-racist, post-white supremacist society, we would have to acknowledge that:

1. Ethnicity refers to one's culture(s).

2. The concept of racial difference and whiteness ("race") is a social construct whose sole purpose has been to divide human beings and to maintain white supremacy, i.e. the status quo.

3. Although there are black and brown cultures (ethnicities), there is no black or brown race.

4. Although there are white cultures (ethnicities), there is no white race.

5. The idea of people being "biracial" or "multiracial" is an outcome of the sociocultural construct of race.

6. Being "white" should not automatically entitle anyone to privilege, protection or power, or to feel that he/she is the "norm," the "standard," or "superior" in any way to anyone else of a darker skin tone.

7. Being "black" or "brown" should not endanger anyone's safety or prospects, or subject anyone to demeaning or offensive treatment or cause him/her to feel inferior.

8. The "one-drop rule" must be eradicated and be seen for what it is, a fraudulent social and legal

principle of racial classification meant to divide and conquer human beings, maintain a system of white supremacy and deny individuals their wholeness.

9. There is absolutely no scientific basis for the notion of "racial purity." All people alive today are descended from common ancestors who lived millions of years ago in Africa. Human beings, of every hue, are closely related.

10. Being educated on these specific matters is a crucial step toward confronting the fallacy of whiteness and racial difference.

It is anything but naïve to tackle racial injustice at its root. Quite the opposite—it is transformative. Without an intentional, conscious reeducation and redefinition of ourselves and of our society, future generations will be powerless to think, or act differently than we currently do. The vicious cycle will only continue.

My brother Nicky Enright concludes his "Break The Cycle" essay with the following statement, "To transform this country we must confront this painful history, expose it, and differentiate it from the present and future. That would be radical—and healing."

Radical transformation and laying a new foundation that will allow for healing and true systemic change is exactly what this society needs. ✿

TWENTY-FOUR

The Power of One

AS HUMAN BEINGS, we tend to minimize the power of our own voices. We often believe that as individuals, we cannot create concrete, long-lasting change. I know I will not necessarily live to witness a cataclysmic shift in how our society challenges systemic racism but I refuse to raise my son adhering to the erroneous and divisive ideology that gave rise to that system and that has allowed it to flourish for generations.

Despite his love for and support of me, I am certain there are times when Adam cannot wholly empathize with my experience, given how he and Sebastián are received in the world when they are without me. But Adam experiences the stares, the curiosity, the questions, and the hostility when he is out in the world with both of us, and though this is not quite the same as what I experience, it gives him an inside look at what racism and a belief in whiteness does to individuals and to a society. He is often angered with the stories I share with him, or with what he himself witnesses, and he is part of the determination to raise our son to know his whole truth and to then be able to see the whole truth of others. There is power in that determination, and change comes about as a result of that determination.

The individuals my family connects with, in some ways are forever changed as a result of meeting our family. I am not saying that they will permanently view racism or our society in a profoundly different way, but a seed has been planted for them to question what our society teaches about "race" and identity.

There are many tangible ways that my family and I have been the change we wish to see. For example, on forms where I have to fill out our "race," I always check every box that applies to Sebastián and me (white, black, Hispanic/Latino, Asian) and when there is the option, I also check "other" and write in "Multiethnic." Even if there is not an option for "other," I add both anyway. As I described in Chapter 14, I did this on the 2010 Census when Sebastián was born and I did it when I registered him at his school. I do not know what happens to these forms once I have submitted them, nor how my son and I are truly categorized by others, but I assert my own power and agency by filling them out in a way that echoes who we truly are. It is a small, but brave act of protest against the language and ideology of racial difference.

When I was a Spanish teacher, I purposely displayed photos of my family, including my mother, so that my students were exposed every day to a family that defied the notion of skin color as definer and as affinity. I remember one student studying a picture of Sebastián one day and nervously, tentatively saying to me, "*Señorita*, can I ask you a question?" I replied, "Of course. What's up?" He then said, "Why is your son so white?" I smiled and chuckled a bit and said, "That's a good question. Well, my husband is of Irish and German ancestry and I'm Russian Jewish on my dad's side and have Spanish ancestry on my mom's side, so my son is mostly European in his heritage, and that's why he looks the way he does. But he still has African and Native American ancestry through me, even though it may not be obviously visible on his face."

My student studied the picture for a few moments more and then responded, "Oh. That's cool. You never know." I smiled. This was an African American and Puerto Rican student, with coloring closer to mine, and I loved that he felt brave enough to ask me about my son's physical appearance. It opened a dialogue about genetic variation, inheritance, and what the world sees versus who we are. I have no doubt that the conversation impacted my student, and that it may have influenced how he views others as well as how he views himself.

We have lived in the same home and neighborhood since before Sebastián was born, and are familiar to many of the local business owners and employees. Sebastián and I have developed relationships with many of these individuals, and they all know Sebastián is bilingual and that he is my biological son. Many in fact have met my mother and even knew my father. And they of course know Adam.

Recently, one of those individuals said something very powerful to me. She is Dominican American, so when we see her, Sebastián and I always speak to her in Spanish. She sometimes babysits one of Sebastián's preschool classmates and told me of an exchange she had that made her think of us. A mother at the playground gave her a message to give to the mother of her charge, Sebastián's preschool classmate, who is white. This woman we know is dark-skinned. She said she nodded to the message but that she instantly thought of me, and how this woman had presumed she was the boy's nanny solely because of their different skin colors. She said she thought about how that happens to me all the time with Sebastián, who is my child. She said that although in her case the woman was right that she was the caretaker, and not the mother, it was wrong of her to approach with that assumption and even worse, to act upon that assumption.

In November 2017, I attended a Celebration of Life gathering to honor Gus Trowbridge, the co-founder of Manhattan Country School, at The Cathedral of St. John the Divine. He died in July 2017. It was an incredibly moving and beautiful ceremony. Gus Trowbridge truly was the change he wished to see, and he is a shining example of the power one individual can have. The Cathedral was full of people he had impacted for over fifty years, some of whom had attended MCS in the 1970s and some, like me, who had taught there.

After the ceremony, there was a reception, which in many ways was a reunion for people who had not seen each other for years, in some cases for decades. I hugged and chatted with many former students, their families, and former colleagues, and had an exchange with one that validated the way Adam and I are raising Sebastián.

Many of these individuals had known me when I was pregnant and knew Sebastián as a baby and as a toddler. When I showed them pictures, they were shocked to see the big boy he had become. Many asked me if he speaks Spanish, and I proudly responded that yes, he is completely bilingual and attends a dual language school. One former colleague, a bilingual Dominican American said to me, "I always think about how you would speak to Sebastián only in Spanish, not worrying about what others would think or even how others would feel. I really respected that and it's inspired me to teach my own future children Spanish. It is so beautiful to know your family's language, and seeing what you have done with your son, inspires me to do the same. It's important for children to know all of who they are."

My heart was full of appreciation for her words. In that brief exchange, she validated the choices I have made as a mother and the positive impact it has had and continues to have on my son.

I nearly cried when she said that to me because more often than not my motherhood is questioned or challenged, but in that moment, it was seen and respected. That is creating change.

Despite all of the naysayers or doubters, there are many individuals who have expressed to me their respect and admiration for how Adam and I are raising our son. Many people have told me that I am brave for resisting the status quo, particularly in regards to my son. Those who truly wish to understand what I am doing with regards to my son and what I hope to do with regards to my work, understand that not only does systemic racism outrage me, but the foundation that created that system outrages me. Those individuals understand that I am truly antiracist and that the work I am doing is genuine antiracism. Being told that I am bold and fearless validates my role as a mother and my role as an antiracist activist. I need that validation – it is part of what propels me to continue speaking our truth.

The work of antiracism requires an absolute rejection of the language and ideology of racial difference and whiteness. We cannot claim to be antiracist while accepting (and perpetuating) the fallacies of racial difference and whiteness. Accepting and perpetuating both only empowers systemic racism and white supremacy.

Sebastián has observed my fearlessness and conviction his entire life and it has deeply affected his own self-identification and boldness. Sebastián recently told Adam and me that his skin color is "peach brown." We looked at each other, wide-eyed and smiled, because honestly, not only is it a perfect description, it illustrates his understanding that he is a blend of us as well as his love for and closeness to people with darker skin than his own. He sees himself in me and in my side of the family, so he is finding language that describes his own truth.

Sebastián also shared this description with his second grade teacher and classmates during a discussion about identity. His teacher told me that he emphatically let everyone know that he is not "white" and that his statement about being "peach brown" led to a further examination about "whether or not color represents who we are and how we identify." His teacher sharing that exchange with me was music to my ears. Adam and I both (and our families) could not have been more proud. I will not deny that I am tempted to write in "peach brown" for him on the 2020 Census.

In August 2016, Sebastián and I traveled to visit one of my closest friends from high school and her children in Colorado. It was my first time flying alone with my son, and I felt extremely nervous about how we would be viewed and treated as we traveled through very different parts of the country. I was certain we would be stared at, but I worried about someone intervening, thinking I did not have the right to be with this "white" child, or perhaps people voicing their racism toward us. It ended up being fairly uneventful, but Sebastián and I both had exchanges during our layover in Dallas that revealed how destructive an ideology of racial difference and whiteness is.

As we stepped off our plane in Dallas, I felt anxious, not knowing the airport and knowing we had to make a connecting flight to Denver. I approached an airport employee to ask where our gate was. She looked at my son and me disdainfully and literally turned her back on me, ignoring my question completely. I was incensed and felt the blood rushing to my face. I angrily responded, "Thanks for nothing" and walked on, finding the gate on my own. Sebastián observed this moment, and looked upset about it himself, though he did not say anything to me. I could read, though, that it upset him to see his mother so easily disrespected.

I was still seething with fury as we entered our gate, carrying a car seat and our luggage. As we sat down, Sebastián noticed a little girl and her family right next to us. I had caught them eyeing us as we entered and found a place to sit, and had a good idea about their thought processes, but I was already upset enough about that employee that I decided to ignore them. Sebastián, however, seeing a little girl close to his age, decided to engage.

As Sebastián and I had found our gate, we were speaking to each other in Spanish, and the little girl and her family overheard us. After Sebastián approached the little girl, asking her name or age, I do not remember, she gave him a disdainful and dismissive look and said harshly, "I talk English." I felt my heart palpitate with anger, this time even more powerfully because of its potential effect on my son. Before I could intervene, however, Sebastián matter-of-factly, responded, "I talk English and Spanish." My anger quickly turned into pride. My son was stating his truth, and though he could not fully comprehend the weight of the girl's statement (nor could she, sadly), he was defending himself and that truth. I then did intervene, telling Sebastián in Spanish, to ignore the little girl as she was not being friendly and did not deserve his attention. He happily complied.

Both of those exchanges, however, revealed the extremity to which white people have internalized their supposed inherent superiority. That white airport employee and that white little girl were simply manifesting the lessons they have been absorbing their entire lives—about mattering more than black and brown people, as well as the illusion that they are inherently different from black and brown people. The employee did not see me—she saw a brown face that she felt did not merit or deserve her attention. And that little girl heard another language that in her mind also did not merit or deserve her attention.

I was very upset by these two exchanges, but I was also proud to see how my son and I both responded. In some ways, I was prouder of Sebastián. I have had a lifetime of dismissal and disrespect, and the narrative of racial difference, says that I as a brown woman will experience racism. But my son, despite being presumed to be white, is not only also experiencing racism, he is responding to it proactively, in a way that challenges the system as well as the narrative.

As my brother Nicky states in his essay, "I know racism intimately, as an oppressive force, as most people of color do in America. Sadly, I have had no shortage of racist encounters in my life while in the pursuit of my regular affairs and dreams. Consequently, in saying that race is a fiction, I by no means wish to imply that racism is a fiction. That would be naïve indeed. But it is a crucial distinction, without which, we remain locked in a cycle."(Enright, 2016, 3) James Baldwin reaffirms this idea when he said:

> "Therefore, whatever white people do not know about Negroes reveals, precisely and inexorably, what they do not know about themselves. This denial—and anyone who accepts the status quo is guilty of it—is as corrosive as hatred. It is corrosive because it requires purposeful blindness." (Baldwin, 1992, 38)

That purposeful blindness is precisely what has allowed the ideology of racial difference and whiteness to go forth, unchallenged, and as a result, what has allowed systemic racism and white supremacy to go forth with impunity.

We should all refuse to participate in that purposeful blindness. We need to envision a new reality. But we cannot envision a new reality unless we open our eyes.

As we continue to challenge and I hope to dismantle white supremacy and systemic racism, let us rewrite the narrative of who we are. We are not inherently different from each other based on skin color, and our skin tone does not reveal who we are.

Our stories are not written on our faces. ✳

BIBLIOGRAPHY

Achebe, Chinua. *Things Fall Apart.* Nigeria: William Heinemann Ltd., 1958.

Baldwin, James. "On Being White ... And Other Lies," *Essence Magazine,* April 1984: 135-136. https://groups.google.com/forum/#!topic/yclsa-eom-forum/jHoel-YdkM4 (accessed on January 24, 2019).

Baldwin, James. n.d. video, 0:10, https://www.youtube.com/watch?v=DUknb68MWLE (accessed January 19, 2019).

Baldwin, James (1963), *The Fire Next Time.* New York: Vintage, 1992

Biss, Eula. "White Debt." *The New York Times Magazine,* December 2, 2015. https://www.nytimes.com/2015/12/06/magazine/white-debt.html?login=smartlock&auth=login-smartlock (accessed January 22, 2019).

Chen, Chih-Yuan. *Gugi, Gugi.* California: Kane/Miller Book Publishers, Inc., 2004

Chakiris, George, Betty Wand, vocalists. "America," music by Leonard Bernstein, lyrics by Stephen Sondheim, recorded August 9, 1960, track 7 on *West Side Story* (Original Motion Picture Soundtrack), Columbia Vinyl LP, 1961.

Clark, Dr. Kenneth B. and Mamie Phipps. *Racial Identification And Preference in Negro Children. Doll Study, 1940s.* https://i2.cdn. turner.com/cnn/2010/images/05/13/doll.study.1947.pdf (accessed January 25, 2019).

Coates, Ta-Nehisi. *Between the World and Me.* New York: Spiegel & Grau, 2015.

Coates, Ta-Nehisi. foreword to *The Origin of Others,* xii-xvii. Authored by Toni Morrison. Cambridge: Harvard University Press, 2017.

Díaz, Junot. *The Brief Wondrous Life of Oscar Wao.* New York: Riverhead Books, 2007.

Enright, Nicky. "Race Through The Census," 2013 http://www. lightbolt.net/source_files/pages/2d/Race-thru-Census.html (accessed January 18, 2019).

Enright, Nicky. "Break The Cycle." May 2016. http://www.lightbolt. net/source_files/pages/Texts/Break-the-Cycle-Nicky-Enright. pdf (accessed January 18, 2019).

Finding Your Roots with Henry Louis Gates Jr. 2012-present. Produced by Kunhardt McGee Productions, Inkwell Films, Ark Media. United States: PBS. Television.

Gregg, Carl. "What Ta-Nehisi Coates Taught Me About 'People Who Believe They Are White.'" *Patheos, S*eptember 24, 2015. https:// www.patheos.com/blogs/carlgregg/2015/09/what-ta-nehisi-coates-taught-me-about-people-who-believe-they-are-white/ (accessed January 24, 2019).

Hoyt, Carlos A. Jr. *The Arc of a Bad Idea: Understanding and Transcending Race.* Oxford, United Kingdom: Oxford University Press, 2016.

Hurston. Zora Neale (1937), *Their Eyes Were Watching God.* Illinois: University of Illinois Press, 1991.

Kolbert, Elizabeth. "THE RACE ISSUE, There's No Scientific Basis for Race—It's a Made-Up Label." *National Geographic,* April 2018. https://www.nationalgeographic.com/magazine/2018/04/race-genetics-science-africa/ (accessed January 18, 2019).

La Historia Oficial. Directed by Luis Puenzo. 1985; Argentina: Almi Pictures/Koch Lorber Films. Film.

Lorde, Audre. *Sister Outsider: Essays and Speeches.* Berkeley: Crossing Press, 2007.

Martin, Ann M. *The Babysitters Club Series.* New York: Scholastic Corporation, 1986-2000.

McIntosh, Peggy. "White Privilege: Unpacking the Invisible Knapsack." *Peace and Freedom Magazine,* July/August 1989, 10-12 https://nationalseedproject.org/Key-SEED-Texts/white-privilege-unpacking-the-invisible-knapsack (accessed January 25, 2019).

Miller, Lisa. "Can Racism Be Stopped in the Third Grade?." *New York Magazine,* May 19, 2015. http://nymag.com/scienceofus/2015/05/can-fieldston-un-teach-racism.html (accessed January 22, 2019).

Norris, Michelle. *The Race Card Project.* National Public Radio (NPR), 2010-Present https://theracecardproject.com/ (accessed on January 25, 2019)

El Norte. Directed by Gregory Nava. 1983; United States/United Kingdom: Cinecom International, PBS. Film.

Norton, Quinn. "How White People Got Made, Part Two of a Series on Whiteness (Part One)." *The Message on the Medium,* October 17, 2014. https://medium.com/message/how-white-people-got-made-6eeb076ade42 (accessed January 18, 2019).

Nye, Bill. "Rutgers University Commencement Speech." Speech presented at Rutgers University, High Point Solutions Stadium in Piscataway, NJ, May 17, 2015.

Orjoux, Alanne, Paul P. Murphy and Ray Sanchez. "Attorney in rant that went viral says he's not a racist and offers an apology." *CNN,* May 22, 2018. https://www.cnn.com/2018/05/22/us/aaron-schlossberg-attorney-racist-rant-apology/index.html (accessed January 18, 2018).

Oxford Academic (Oxford University Press). "Non-Racial Identities and Worldviews, The Racialization Process and The History of Race and Racialization," video, 3:13, April 2016, featuring of Carlos A. Hoyt Jr. https://www.youtube.com/watch?v=i1GjU01AMjE (accessed January 24, 2019).

Painter, Nell Irvin. *The History of White People.* New York: W.W. Norton & Company, 2010

Pascal, Francine. *Sweet Valley High Series.* New York: Penguin Random House, 1983-2003

Rankine, Claudia. *Citizen: An American Lyric.* Minnesota: Graywolf Press, 2014

Rich, Adrienne. "Invisibility in Academe," *Blood, Bread, and Poetry: Selected Prose, 1979-1985.* New York: W.W. Norton & Company, Inc., 1986.

Rich, Nathaniel. "James Baldwin & the Fear of a Nation." *The New York Review of Books,* May 12, 2016. http://kalamu.com/neogriot/2016/05/17/review-essay-james-baldwin-the-fear-of-a-nation/ (accessed January 24, 2019).

Rodgers, Richard and Oscar Hammerstein II. "You've Got to Be Carefully Taught." New York: Williamson Music Inc, 1949.

Santayana, George. *The Life of Reason: Reason in Common Sense.* New York: Scribner's, 1905: 284.

Seuss, Dr. The Sneetches And Other Stories. New York: Penguin Random House, 1953

Stand and Deliver. Directed by Ramón Menéndez. 1988; United States: Warner Bros. Film.

Stevenson, Bryan, "Did Slavery End in 1865?" Equal Justice Institute, August 19, 2016 video, 3:49, https://portside.org/equal-justice-institute (accessed January 19, 2019).

Sugar. Directed by Anna Boden and Ryan Fleck. 2008; United States: Sony Pictures Classics Axiom Films. Film.

Trowbridge, Augustus. *Begin With a Dream: How a Private School with a Public Mission Changed the Politics of Race, Class and Gender in American Education.* Indiana: Xlibris, 2005.

Tsui, Bonnie, "Choose Your Own Identity," *The New York Times Magazine,* December 14, 2015 https://www.nytimes.com/2015/12/14/magazine/choose-your-own-identity.html (accessed January 22, 2019).

Wang, Amy B. "Two Americans were detained by a Border Patrol agent after he heard them speaking Spanish." *The Washington Post,* May 21, 2018. https://www.washingtonpost.com/news/post-nation/wp/2018/05/20/a-border-patrol-agent-detained-two-u-s-citizens-at-a-gas-station-after-hearing-them-speak-spanish/?noredirect=on&utm_term=.334d44f4caf0 (accessed January 18, 2018).

Williams, Thomas Chatterton. "Black and Blue and Blond." *VQR Magazine,* Winter 2015. https://www.vqronline.org/essays-articles/2015/01/black-and-blue-and-blond (accessed on January 25, 2019)

Yamato, Gloria. "Something About the Subject Makes It Hard To Name," in *Race, Class, and Gender,* Margaret L. Anderson and Patricia Hill Collins, eds. Belmont, California: Thomson Wadsworth Publishing, 2004: 99-103.

PHOTO: Adam Whittaker

ABOUT THE AUTHOR

NAOMI RAQUEL ENRIGHT was born to a Jewish American father and an Ecuadorian mother in La Paz, Bolivia. She is a native English and Spanish speaker, and was raised in New York City. She taught Spanish for eight years, and worked as a diversity practitioner for three years, where she became a National SEED (Seeking Educational Equity and Diversity) Facilitator. Her essay, "From One Exile to Another," appeared in *The Beiging of America: Personal Narratives About Being Mixed Race in the 21st Century* (2017). She has also published essays in *Hold The Line Magazine, Family Story Project,* and *Role Reboot.* She has a blog where she writes about the ideology of racial difference, challenging systemic racism, grief/loss and parenting. Enright holds a BA in Anthropology from Kenyon College and studied at the Universidad de Sevilla in Spain her junior year. She resides with her family in Brooklyn, New York. ❀

OTHER BOOKS BY 2LEAF PRESS

2Leaf Press challenges the status quo by publishing alternative fiction, non-fiction, poetry and bilingual works by activists, academics, poets and authors dedicated to diversity and social justice with scholarship that is accessible to the general public. 2Leaf Press produces high quality and beautifully produced hardcover, paperback and ebook formats through our series: 2LP Explorations in Diversity, 2LP University Books, 2LP Classics, 2LP Translations, Nuyorican World Series, and 2LP Current Affairs, Culture & Politics. Below is a selection of 2Leaf Press' published titles.

2LP EXPLORATIONS IN DIVERSITY

Substance of Fire: Gender and Race in the College Classroom
by Claire Millikin
Foreword by R. Joseph Rodríguez, Afterword by Richard Delgado
Contributors Riley Blanks, Blake Calhoun, Rox Trujillo

Black Lives Have Always Mattered
A Collection of Essays, Poems, and Personal Narratives
Edited by Abiodun Oyewole

The Beiging of America:
Personal Narratives about Being Mixed Race in the 21st Century
Edited by Cathy J. Schlund-Vials, Sean Frederick Forbes, Tara Betts
Afterword by Heidi Durrow

What Does it Mean to be White in America?
Breaking the White Code of Silence, A Collection of Personal Narratives
Edited by Gabrielle David and Sean Frederick Forbes
Introduction by Debby Irving, Afterword by Tara Betts

2LP UNIVERSITY BOOKS
Designs of Blackness, Mappings in the Literature and Culture of African Americans
by A. Robert Lee
20TH ANNIVERSARY EXPANDED EDITION

2LP CLASSICS
Adventures in Black and White
by Philippa Schuyler
Edited and with a critical introduction by Tara Betts

Monsters: Mary Shelley's Frankenstein and Mathilda
by Mary Shelley, edited by Claire Millikin Raymond

2LP TRANSLATIONS
Birds on the Kiswar Tree
by Odi Gonzales, translated by Lynn Levin
Bilingual: English/Spanish

Incessant Beauty, A Bilingual Anthology
by Ana Rossetti, edited and translated by Carmela Ferradáns
Bilingual: English/Spanish

NUYORICAN WORLD SERIES
Entre el sol y la nieve: escritos de fin de siglo / Between the Sun and Snow: Writing at the End of the Century
by Myna Nieves, translated by Christopher Hirschmann Brandt
Bilingual: English/Spanish

Our Nuyorican Thing, The Birth of a Self-Made Identity
by Samuel Carrion Diaz, Introduction by Urayoán Noel

Hey Yo! Yo Soy!, 40 Years of Nuyorican Street Poetry, The Collected Works of Jesús Papoleto Meléndez
Bilingual: English/Spanish

LITERARY NONFICTION
No Vacancy; Homeless Women in Paradise
by Michael Reid

The Beauty of Being, A Collection of Fables, Short Stories & Essays
by Abiodun Oyewole

*WHEREABOUTS: Stepping Out of Place, An Outside in Literary &
Travel Magazine Anthology*
Edited by Brandi Dawn Henderson

ESSAYS
The Emergence of Ecosocialism, Collected Essays by Joel Kovel
Edited by Quincy Saul

PLAYS
Rivers of Women, The Play
by Shirley Bradley LeFlore, photographs by Michael J. Bracey

AUTOBIOGRAPHIES/MEMOIRS/BIOGRAPHIES
*An Unintentional Accomplice:
A Personal Perspective on White Responsibility*
by Carolyn L. Baker

*Trailblazers, Black Women Who Helped Make America Great
American Firsts/American Icons, Vols. 1 and 2*
by Gabrielle David, Introduction by Chandra D. L. Waring, Edited
by Carolina Fung Feng

*Mother of Orphans
The True and Curious Story of Irish Alice, A Colored Man's Widow*
by Dedria Humphries Barker
Introduction by Cathy J. Schlund-Vials

Strength of Soul
by Naomi Raquel Enright

*Dream of the Water Children:
Memory and Mourning in the Black Pacific*

by Fredrick D. Kakinami Cloyd
Foreword by Velina Hasu Houston, Introduction by Gerald Horne
Edited by Karen Chau

The Fourth Moment: Journeys from the Known to the Unknown, A Memoir
by Carole J. Garrison, Introduction by Sarah Willis

POETRY

Ransom Street, Poems by Claire Millikin
Introduction by Kathleen Ellis

Wounds Fragments Derelict, Poems by Carlos Gabriel Kelly
Introduction by Sean Frederick Forbes

PAPOLíTICO, Poems of a Political Persuasion
by Jesús Papoleto Meléndez
with an Introduction by Joel Kovel and DeeDee Halleck

Critics of Mystery Marvel, Collected Poems
by Youssef Alaoui, Introduction by Laila Halaby

shrimp
by jason vasser-elong, Introduction by Michael Castro

The Revlon Slough, New and Selected Poems
by Ray DiZazzo, Introduction by Claire Millikin

A Country Without Borders: Poems and Stories of Kashmir
by Lalita Pandit Hogan, Introduction by Frederick Luis Aldama

2Leaf Press Inc. is a nonprofit organization that publishes and promotes multicultural literature.

FLORIDA ■ NEW YORK
www.2leafpress.org